Effective Meetings

The Complete Guide

EFFECTIVE MEETINGS
THE COMPLETE GUIDE

Clyde W. Burleson

WILEY

John Wiley & Sons, Inc.
New York • Chichester • Brisbane • Toronto • Singapore

Library of Congress Cataloging-in-Publication Data

Burleson, Clyde W., 1934-
    Effective meetings : the complete guide / Clyde W. Burleson.
      p.   cm.
    Includes bibliographical references.
    ISBN 0-471-50844-6. — ISBN 0-471-50843-8 (pbk.)
    1. Meetings—Handbooks, manuals, etc. I. Title.
AS6.B86 1990
658.4'56—dc20   89-22452
                                          CIP

Printed in the United States of America

10 9 8 7 6 5 4 3

Contents

Introduction

No one really knows how many hours are actually spent in meetings each year. A recent survey of 2000 business leaders indicated that managers are spending more time in meetings than five years ago. Some managers estimate 70 percent of their average day is spent in meetings. That figure doesn't include hours used preparing for meetings, analyzing the results of meetings, and scheduling new meetings. All this occurs in spite of the fact that the same study indicated that managers felt that about one-third of those meetings are unproductive leading to an estimated $37 billion a year in wasted time.

Meetings continue to be held because they are essential to an organization's success. Your ability to conduct productive meetings is essential to your success.

Meetings range in size from a few individuals conferring in a small office to gatherings with over a thousand participants in an expensive resort hotel. Big or small, effective meetings, those in which a spark ignites an exchange that produces exciting ideas and solutions, are rare. Such meetings are rare because the spark seldom ignites accidentally.

This book is a guide to producing the sparks that make meetings worthwhile.

Worthwhile meetings take place because someone brings together the right mixture of proper timing, physical factors, preparation, and people skills. Good meetings depend upon attention to detail and correct participation by all attendees, including the group leader.

1

Although meeting skills are crucial for managerial advancement there is a woeful lack of formal training in the skills needed to plan, schedule, and conduct effective meetings. You can be one of the few able to hold exceptional meetings and, in turn, reap personal as well as professional benefits.

HOW TO USE THIS BOOK

This book deals with the important meeting skills, including those used in the new and growing field of electronic conferencing.

To get the most from this book, read it from cover to cover. Highlight points you deem interesting. Make margin notes—especially when you can relate the information to a real-life experience.

Once you've been through the book and have an overall feeling for what is offered, single out those chapters that will enable you to deal with your specific problem areas. Reread these sections.

Select one technique from your second perusal and use it. Analyse the results, then add another as soon as the first has become automatic.

Finally, keep this book handy for a reference as well as a motivation to improve your meeting abilities. After a little practical experience, you will be adding your own ideas. You'll be one of the best informed meeters around.

WHO CAN HOLD GOOD MEETINGS?

To hold good meetings, you don't have to be the gregarious, hearty, extroverted, hail-and-well-met type, nor do you have to be an entertainer or even a particularly inspiring leader. All it takes is an understanding of how and why meetings work or fail and the ability to be yourself.

In the next few meetings you attend, watch the chairperson. Chances are, this individual will alter his or her personality to fit a personal stereotyped image of leadership behavior. This is a serious error.

Be yourself, as an attendee or as a chairperson. You'll accomplish more, because others in the meeting can quickly detect role-playing and don't know how to react. Even worse, role-playing is catching and places every discussion on false ground, assuring no decisive action.

THE MEETING MANDATE

This Meeting Mandate is discussed later in detail, but is so important it deserves repetition:

KNOW WHAT YOU WANT FROM A MEETING.

Attending a meeting without a clear notion of what you want to accomplish is an exercise in futility. If you don't know what you want going in, your chances of getting it aren't just limited; they are reduced to near zero. In addition, not knowing what you want from a meeting makes you a participant without a purpose. You become a floating head-nodder or human rubberstamp on whatever action those leading the group determine to take.

If you come away from this book with nothing else, understand that going into a meeting, no matter how well prepared otherwise, without a clear, definable notion of what you want to accomplish, is a disservice to you, your organization, and your future. To remain competetive in this global economy, businesspeople must become more productive and strive for new levels of excellence. Improvement in your meeting skills will bring these must-attain goals closer.

1 | Meeting Mania: To Meet or Not to Meet

With apologies to Shakespeare: To meet or not to meet, that is the question. This question is seldom asked, yet holding fewer meetings results in lower overhead, lessened workload, and increased productivity, not to mention improved company morale.

Meeting mania is a problem that all managers need to address.

One of the biggest contributors to over-meeting is laziness. It is easier for most managers to spend an hour and a half in a meeting as opposed to half an hour writing or dictating a report covering the same elements. Written reports have advantages. People are generally more careful about what they write than what they say. Written reports tend to have more exact information and less reaction to personalities.

Written reports are not in the scope of this book, however, and the decision remains whether to meet or not to meet.

IS THIS MEETING NECESSARY?

An unnecessary meeting will never be a good one. There might be some fine jokes passed around and the latest company gossip can get a workout, but if those in attendance know the meeting isn't really necessary, nothing is going to be accomplished. It is a bust before it begins.

5

A meeting that's barely necessary doesn't fare much better. Such meetings often involve more people than needed; a memo or one-on-one conversation would have sufficed, saving both time and money.

The first question you have to ask yourself, before proposing a meeting, is as follows:

IS THIS MEETING REALLY NECESSARY?

A "maybe" response indicates only limited need for the meeting and shows that further thought is required. Only a "yes" is a positive justification for calling a meeting.

The same question needs to be asked before attending a meeting.

If the meeting is not necessary and you can avoid it, do so. If you have to attend, try to use the time to shorten your workload to compensate for the lost hours.

Many managers find it hard to judge if a meeting is needed or superfluous. There are some guidelines which are revealing:

1. Is the meeting being called to exchange information or viewpoints?

If the meeting is to discuss viewpoints, it is probably a necessary conference. If the meeting is strictly to distribute information, the meeting is probably unnecessary. Meetings are most effective when used to find solutions or resolutions to conflicts.

A meeting held for the sole purpose of imparting information had better have some pretty spectacular revelations. This, in all likelihood, should be classed as an inspirational conference, because important news is seldom passed along without editorializing or explanations. Inspirational meetings are difficult to conduct, because they are based on emotion, but there are times when the troops need boosting or, conversely, deflating.

Training meetings appear to be an exception to the don't-meet-to-exchange-information concept. They are not. Distributing information in advance allows the meeting to be used for developing concepts and testing individual understanding. This is a better use of everyone's time. This is not to downplay the importance of instructional sessions. It is just to set this category of communications apart from other meetings.

Some meetings seem to be for information and opinions. When this is the case, it is less than optimum to give individuals new information and expect honest evaluation and expert comments in a group environment. Most people want time to think through their opinions before sharing them.

Information, facts, figures, sales data, market intelligence, production numbers, personnel reviews, and more, can be disseminated more effectively by memo than meeting. Chances are, the memo is going to be written anyway and passed out at the meeting. Distributing a memo is okay if there is other business on hand, but calling a meeting solely as a means of handing paper to other managers is inappropriate.

Meetings are at their best when used to generate expressions of viewpoints or concepts, or to develop policy.

Meetings are at their worst when used to check individual progress on various projects. There are few more mind-dulling experiences than to sit at a conference table and hear about the status of tasks that are not even remotely connected with yours. These sessions often turn into excuse contests with rambling dissertations on the reasons behind delays or problems.

In summary, meetings are generally not an efficient way to dispense information. If that is the primary reason for the gathering, then rethink the need for convening.

2. Can one-on-one conversations or even one-on-two conversations accomplish what needs to be done? Or is a larger group necessary?

There is a difference between a meeting and a conversation between two or three people. A conversation is relaxed, informal, and rarely has the time constraints posed by a meeting. Those present sense the difference.

Decisions are rarely made in conversations. In fact, some managers and executives become agitated when two or three members of a committee converse and come to a consensus without the others present. This nervousness is not assuaged by a follow-up memo which details the conversation or even by the fact that the decision may be nothing more than a unified front, in no way binding upon the group.

Paranoia is, to some degree, part of the business environment. Meetings get called to relieve this disturbing feeling of suspicion.

It is possible, in many cases, to ease anxiety by informing others of the conversation and even inviting them to attend. Be careful, though, because such invitations are liable to be accepted, and what was supposed to be an informal talk becomes a mini-meeting.

If conversation will suffice to avoid another meeting, then have the talk. Inform the other committee members or interested parties. Those smart enough to advance in management will welcome one less meeting on their schedule.

3. Is this meeting being called because someone or some group doesn't have enough to do?

It happens all the time. Workloads in an organization can be un-balanced. This week, Production has more than it can handle, while Sales is coasting. One way to fill the day for Sales is to call a meeting. This is more common than anyone dares admit.

4. Is the agenda for the called-meeting vague? Or worse, is there no agenda at all?

Agendas are covered in Chapter 4. As a basic rule of meeting-skill, do not go to a meeting where there is no agenda. If you have to attend, go prepared for the worst.

If a manager cannot express on paper what the meeting is about, there probably shouldn't be a meeting at all.

If you are asked to a meeting and no agenda is given to you in advance, find the person who called the meeting and ask for one. If it is verbal, take notes.

Many times, the person discovers he or she has vague ideas about why the meeting is needed. This experience can benefit both of you.

5. Is there any reason to meet other than the fact that your group has a set, regular, once-a-week mandatory meeting?

For example, top management often wants certain employees to get together each and every week, to discuss items of importance, or to match timing, balance workloads, and do ongoing, necessary house-keeping.

After a few sessions, these meetings fall into a routine and small talk dominates.

The reason the meeting time and date were set in advance was to allow everyone to clear schedules to accommodate the session. The meeting is mandatory so every participant must be there . . . every time.

Does this really work? Yes and no. Repeatedly, one or more members are missing and send substitutes, who cannot act in the absent member's place. The substitute is a human recording machine, inserted to bring back news of what happened. News is brought back, all right, but because the attendee wasn't at past sessions, the report is often a garbled, mess which takes another meeting to straighten out.

Are mandatory, fixed-time-and-date conferences worthless? Not at all. Neither are they a way for a manager to get the most from every staff member.

The regular meeting should be set and individual schedules cleared. Then the day before, the manager should do a little checking. Is there actually a need to convene? Could a more limited gathering accomplish the same things? Would a memo suffice? Could matters be handled by a phone call? If the answer is yes, skip the meeting.

Experience has shown that attendance at called-meetings set up in this fashion is better than for the regular meeting which is held without exception.

Some managers assigned to the no-excuse meeting bring other work they can do. They listen just enough to know when their attention is needed.

If you are part of such a group, see what you can do to keep it on everyone's schedule as a regular event, yet let necessity determine if and how it happens. Another time-saver is to structure the agenda so individuals are excused for other duties until they are needed in the session.

One guideline should be clear: The only solution to meeting mania is more stringent evaluation of the need to meet, prior to calling a meeting.

MEETINGS COST MONEY

It is difficult to evaluate the actual cost of a meeting because of the time spent before and after meetings. As an example, assume 8 people each prepare for the session for a half hour, meet for an hour, then use a half hour more in evaluation and meeting-generated work. That's 2 hours times 8 people or 16 people-hours. If they each make, say, $40,000, work 48 weeks a year (two off for vacation, two off for personal days and holidays, which is rather standard), their earnings are about $20 per hour. Add another $10 for company benefits, and the meeting costs $480. Ten meetings a day in that organization with higher and lower earners, five days a week, ends up costing $125,000,000 a year of after-tax money—more than a pittance. This may be a good investment if the meetings achieved their purpose, a waste if they do not. In a major organization, total annual meeting costs are incalculable.

Ego Meetings

What about the manager who purports to believe the only way to get information from subordinates is by meeting? This manager may be seeking ego satisfaction. Meetings are not for holding court. It may be a pleasant way to get reports, but it is far from efficient. Any career-minded individual caught in such a situation needs to seriously consider his or her position and prospects.

Evaluate your meeting schedule. If a memo will serve, write a memo. If an informal conversation will work, converse. If a meeting is the only, or best, solution, hold a meeting, but make sure it is a good one.

Avoid being caught in the meeting cycle. Help stamp out meeting mania. Don't be part of the problem.

THE MEETING MANDATE: KNOW WHAT YOU WANT FROM A MEETING

You must never, under any circumstance, attend a meeting without a clear concept of exactly what you want from that meeting.

If you have time to prepare, you can set several goals. If you are called into the meeting without prior notice, then begin goal setting as soon after the meeting begins as possible. If you are the first scheduled presenter, which leaves zero moments for thought of anything except the presentation, do your presentation. Then begin to define what you want from the session. There is nothing wrong with altering your stance later. You can also redirect some of the points you decided upon to achieve another goal.

Knowing what you want isn't self-serving. All those attending the meeting should know what they want, too. That way, positions can be quickly communicated.

Knowing what you want from a meeting does not mean "looking good" to superiors or dominating the discussion. Although knowing what you want will make you look good, because you will be more directed in your statements and responses. Knowing what you want will compel others to listen, because you may well be the only one in the room who has a clear notion of immediate goals.

Knowing what you want does not mean taking a position before the meeting begins and holding that view intransigently, no matter what transpires. It does mean attending each meeting with a purpose.

Few people get into a taxi without a defined destination. Fewer still get on an airplane without some idea of where they are landing and what they will do when they get there.

Yet most people who attend meetings enter the room without any thought of what they want from the meeting. Most executives and managers attend a meeting, form an opinion as the meeting progresses, and then later, decide if that opinion was valid or invalid based on subsequent happenings.

Set a personal goal of attaining what you want from each meeting. A reasonable goal might be to want every fact concerning a situation—the good and the bad, plus the not-so-good and not-so-bad. When you have the facts, you have the basis for rational decision making.

Maybe the meeting has been called to deal with a problem. The information needed is a clear definition of that problem and all solutions suggested to date. That could be your specific goal for this meeting.

Your goal might be to define management's stance on an issue and learn how that stance was developed. This often reveals management's reference to a position taken in an earlier situation which appears similar but, in reality, is quite different.

Your goal might be to classify your fellow attendees on the basis of their positions and develop understanding of why those positions were taken. It might be merely to identify those in the meeting who appear utterly resistant to logic or being swayed.

A realistic goal is to make one single point clear to all others present, or to demonstrate how a series of facts leads to a single conclusion. Your goal may be to introduce a new concept.

Goals are as varied as the purposes for which meetings are called. If you attend without a goal, you will neither contribute your best nor get the most from a meeting.

Goal-setting for getting what you want from a meeting should be a high-priority, formal process. Do not rely on vague notions. You should be able to state your goal succinctly in a sentence or two. Write it out and read it, then edit until it is satisfactory. Work until the goal statement cleanly establishes what you want in return for the time you are about to give to the meeting.

Knowing what you want from a meeting is the key to getting what you want from the meeting without becoming aggressive or demanding or argumentative. Knowing what you want allows single-mindedness and gives purpose to your presence. Knowing what you want from the meeting gives you focus and provides perspective, allowing evaluation of others' positions.

Never, never, under any circumstances, attend a meeting without a clear concept of exactly what you want from that meeting. It's a simple rule. Honored more in its breach, regrettably, that its observation.

2 | Scheduling Your Meeting

Okay, you have decided a meeting is the best answer. You need to call one, or you have been told to call one, and it is your responsibility to get eight people together in the boardroom on Thursday.

That can be a tall order.

Even in a group as small as eight, a couple of people won't see why they are needed. Another one or two won't care, because the meeting is not about a situation that directly concerns them. Some attendees may be easy to schedule because they have nothing else to do. There is sure to be varied interest among the attendees and all are not motivated to be where you want them to be, when you want them there.

MEETING SCHEDULING

Every company has a flow of working hours. Managers arrive about the same time each morning, take an hour to clean up holdover matters and settle into the office routine, then are ready to focus on business of the day.

Most people try to set their meeting according to this or a similar schedule. If managers arrive at 8:00 A.M., then 9:00 A.M. is a popular meeting hour. If work starts at 9:00 A.M., 10:00 A.M. is in demand.

13

Another "natural" time is shortly after lunch. A third is before the final hour of the day, on the basis that this slot allows everyone to "get back to their desks and clear up loose ends" after the meeting.

If the meeting you have to schedule is vital and has everyone's interest, then fitting it into those "natural" time slots won't be hard at all.

Usually, though, competition for prime meeting periods is intense and your need to meet is no greater than someone else's.

The answer is creative scheduling.

THE BREAKFAST MEETING

Just because it's called a "breakfast meeting" doesn't mean breakfast has to be served. Though not mandatory, the availability of juice, coffee, and pastry or a special treat is an added lure for attendees.

Many companies will pay the tab for this kind of breakfast get-together. Others won't but that doesn't mean the cost has to come out of employee pockets. Some firms allow managers to put the charge on their expense account. If there is no company support, even to the extent of furnishing coffee or soft drinks, it is still possible to have refreshments. It just takes a little more time to arrange.

In the memo which schedules the meeting, note that anyone wanting coffee, donuts, or other early repast, should contribute a specific dollar amount to cover expenses. Everyone who extends money will be present. This is one way of guaranteeing attendance.

If you plan a breakfast meeting, add 15 minutes to the time needed to conduct business. That takes care of late arrivals and the human milling around before settling down to matters at hand. Be sure to end promptly, so people can get to their work stations at the usual time.

NOONERS

Another open slot is during lunch. Brown bag is fine.

Start 15 minutes before the usual noon break as an added incentive to attend. It is amazing how many people will respond to an early lunch.

AFTER FIVE

Normal end of the business day may be 5:00 P.M., or 4:00 P.M. or 3:30 P.M., but no matter. Hanging one more meeting onto the end of the day can be a useful technique. Attendees may be tired and therefore slower to react, but this is frequently offset by a more relaxed attitude. People will also want to get things done, so they can end the day.

Before work, at noon, and after work get-togethers have another important feature. Superiors may notice early-comers, late-stayers, and those who dine in at noon. To the person whose boss pays attention to such details, it's a vital lure.

JUGGLING SCHEDULES

Mr. A needs to set a meeting. He calls Ms. B, and 3:00 P.M. is fine with her. He then calls Ms. C, who can't meet at 3:00 P.M. but can convene at 4:00 P.M. He recalls Ms. B, who can't meet at 4:00 P.M., but is open at 9:00 A.M. the following morning. So he calls . . . You know the drill.

The best way to set a meeting is to schedule the next session at the end of the one in progress. "Can everybody get together Wednesday at 8:00 A.M.?" is a question that can be answered by most attendees right then. There is peer pressure against being unavailable, which helps motivate altered schedules.

Be certain before you call for a next meeting that the next meeting is worth having.

The worst way to set a meeting of more than four or five people is by telephone. Whether you do it, or your secretary does it, it takes inordinate time. Not infrequently is a chore that stretches over two or even three days, then begins again when a key person cannot make the date.

One alternative is a "When can we meet?" memo. A sample is shown on page 16.

These memos should be as informal as company policy will allow. Use first names, if possible. A friendly invitation and personal appeal is harder to reject than a formal request.

Ask for help; your fellow managers have been in this same nearly impossible position and know how many hours can be wasted just trying to set a day and time.

Offering to adjust your schedule to accommodate the group makes it that much more difficult for them not to comply.

Do not offer more than one date. There are two possible responses to one date and that's one too many. One date gets a "yes" or "no." If "yeses" outnumber "nos," it is time to convert the "no" group.

To: John, George, Betty, Carl, and Phyllis

Re: Meeting to decide on Ajax matter
We need to get together for an hour as soon as we can.
Please help. You know how difficult it is to get six busy people in the same room. I'll adjust my schedule to meet yours.

Date: Wednesday, April 8, 7:00 A.M.
I'll see if the company will spring for coffee.
Agenda to follow.
Please call my office and leave word.

Thanks,

Don

Contact any who indicate a schedule conflict. See them in person, if possible. If not, use the phone. There are several approaches:

1. *The Boss Ploy.* Let the recalcitrant ones know your boss set the date and time, but do this *only* if it is true. It exerts pressure. This same ploy has variants such as, "It's the only time Jack Kelly (an influential, important client) can make it." The idea is to come up with a force larger than your persuasion, which will be respected enough to alter schedules.

2. *The Left-Out Option.* This works even if there are two individuals who cannot make the date. It does not work for three. "Gee, John. Can't make it, huh? Let's see. Everyone else seems to be able to. Sure you can't?"

If the answer is still negative, add the kicker, "Well, we'll go on without you. I'll fill you in afterwards." The threat of being left out is effective in motivating some managers.

3. *Logic.* "Look, I know it's a pain, but is there any way you can rearrange? This is really important and it's the only time all the rest can get together." Calling on one's sense of being part of a group is another way to exert peer pressure.

Expect to spend time working out schedules. Rely on direct contact, where possible, because it is far more efficient.

EFFECTIVE NOTIFICATION

A late arrival says, "Sorry, I didn't get the word," and the person responsible for setting the meeting can either ignore the implication of inefficiency or stop everything to defend him or herself. Either option is unpleasant.

Defense begins with a three-step notification process. It is a little more effort but will provide the base for a better, more effective gathering.

1. Send a memo to each attendee, stating time, place, and subject under discussion.

2. Call each attendee for verbal confirmation of receipt of your memo. Ask them to mark the time on their appointment schedules.

3. Call again a couple of hours before the meeting, as a reminder. If it's a breakfast get-together, call before the end of work the day before.

If a number of people are involved, make a list and check each name off as the contact is completed. This, plus delivery to attendees of an agenda, listing date, time, and place, ensures everyone is notified.

When you speak with attendees, state the date, time, and place and, if possible, get each to repeat it.

Finally, remind all to be prompt and tell them when the meeting will end. In many ways, meeting scheduling is the hardest meeting skill to learn. It is also one of the most important.

As an exercise, make a list of actions or appeals which would motivate you to attend another person's meeting, even if it meant altering your schedule. Those same appeals will work with others.

3 | Pre-Selling

Knowing what you want from a meeting, before the meeting begins, allows for pre-selling ideas or gaining a precon-sensus of opinion.

Pre-meeting maneuvering is not a shameful practice. It is done, usually informally and with too little forethought, in every company or organization every day.

Pre-selling is one way to make a meeting more effective. By definition, if something can be pre-sold to a majority in a meeting, discussion and consideration of the pre-sold points will be limited. Those points will become "givens."

Successful pre-selling, or developing a consensus before the meeting, may even result in cancellation of meetings.

It is startling how often a group convenes to discuss and consider an already agreed upon position. Maybe this provides a level of security for some, stemming from group approval and hearing the group embrace the position, but what a waste of management time.

WHO TO SELL

The first step in pre-selling is to determine, before the meeting, those who need to be pre-sold.

This group of individuals may espouse a contrary view, be high

19

in management so their acquiescence with your position means almost automatic approval, or be composed of individuals who concur with you in general but differ in specifics.

A PRE-SELLING EXERCISE

Write precisely what you want to achieve at a coming meeting on a sheet of paper. Remember: If it can't be written concisely, it is probably too vague to serve as a goal. Now follow these steps:

∎ List the individuals who will attend the meeting. Rate each, on a scale of 1 to 5, as supportive or unsupportive of your stated goal. One means absolutely against, 5 means totally for.

∎ Single out the opposition. Try to state why each person opposes your goal. Evaluate the reasons. Sometimes, this process alters your feeling about the goal you have established. If so, change it. That's what this step is for—to clarify your goal, make sure it is worthwhile, and to see it through other's eyes.

∎ Single out support. Do the same as you did with the opposition. State why each supports your goal-attainment. This gives you another viewpoint. And may make for adjustments in your goal.

At this point, even with no pre-selling, the exercise has provided benefits far greater than the time it required to complete. The goal has been examined, re-examined, and possibly modified. And your understanding of supporters and opponents has improved.

This procedure gives you information needed for the next step, which is finding a pre-selling approach to supporters and opponents alike.

Are you surprised that pre-selling extends to supporters? Pre-selling those already in agreement locks them into the position. It makes it harder for them to change their minds, therefore, more predictable in their responses.

Evaluate your list again, this time using your knowledge of company politics. Are there any opposition attendees basing their resistance on political grounds? Is any person on the opposite side politically controlling others, causing them to oppose, too? How about the support group? Ask the same questions.

Obviously, leaders of the opposition or support are the prime people to pre-sell.

With the listing done, concentrate on pre-selling. Pre-selling is exactly what the name implies—the use of techniques to alter or reinforce viewpoints before they are expressed to a group in a meeting.

It is not practical to go through this write-it-on-paper procedure for every meeting, but it is a good exercise. Do it often, at first, then, as the ability to sum up attendees' positions grows, save the formal on-paper part for important occasions and as a training check. There is a tendency in all of us to look for easier paths and shortcuts. In this case, the shortcut will also cut short your learning process.

POLITICALLY MOTIVATED POSITIONS

If company politics are going to play a role in the opposition's resistance, then the resistance is intangible and probably emotional. Pre-selling can often detect this bias.

An example of such a situation includes:

∎ A siding with B because B helped A out of a difficult situation

∎ A influencing C to side with B for the same reason, and

∎ D opposing all three, because he or she is against any position supported by the other three

In this mess, the real opponent is B, and it is this individual who needs pre-selling.

It is not Machiavellian, but straight talk can work wonders. Telling someone in private that others are accepting his or her view can open a dialogue or reveal personal enmity. Don't be afraid to hold this conversation, because it usually will be highly informative.

If it becomes clear that politics will play an oppressing role in a meeting, there isn't much you can do. The presence of upper management, unless these are the gamesters playing politics, will sometimes weaken or obliterate the problem. Often, though, nothing will help.

This doesn't mean company politics are all bad. Company politics exist, are a way of life, and must be recognized. Company politics are not the exclusive property of larger firms. Any organization with three or more employees has political activity. It is the effect politics have on your goal attainment, and on meetings you attend, that must be evaluated. When political infighting reduces meeting effectiveness, a disservice is being done to your organization, and to those in the meeting.

Normally, it's the same few people who consistently turn situations into political contests. Get to know those individuals so you can avoid them, because meeting with them is wasteful. If you must meet with someone of this bent, don't do so with the expectation of accomplishing much. And watch your back.

Pre-selling activities will help you identify the habitual politicians.

NO TWO THINK ALIKE

In pre-selling, remember that no two people think exactly alike. Given the same facts, different individuals produce different interpretations. It's a good pre-selling technique to see how others have interpreted situations. You can spot the differences from your views and develop necessary arguments.

SUPERIOR SUPPORT

Pre-selling a superior helps your goal-attainment. One good way to do this, if not used too often, is to see the higher ranking individual before the meeting on another matter, then bring up the meeting and make one good point that will help your situation. Make the point after you get the superior's views, so you can state your case in a manner which will be supportive of his or her thoughts.

PRE-SELLING PITFALLS

Avoid becoming emotional while pre-selling. Emotion has its purpose in a meeting, but in pre-selling, it can make you appear too strongly committed to a position, thus alienating supporters and stubborning detractors.

During your pre-sell, you may suggest a course of action which the person you are trying to influence hasn't considered. That can be good or bad, but opens the mind to other ideas. If you are not the only one pre-selling, you could change supporters into fence-straddlers. There are enough of these, in all meetings, to destroy any desire for creating more.

FACTUAL SUPPORT

If you can find facts to support your position or set a direction which makes your goal more obtainable, use them. Facts are most effective if they're from a disinterested third party, . . . or your competition.

One great way to pre-sell is to find magazine and other articles which espouse your point in some way and distribute them to the meeting attendees. People will read published reports before they listen to an argument from a peer or superior. Reading the information somehow makes it theirs.

LISTENING

Remember the Meeting Mandate: Know what you want from a meeting. Here's another rule of almost equal importance:

Listen!

Listening to the other's point of view starts during pre-selling. Don't switch off when you are through talking, listen . . . understand. If you don't understand, ask questions until you do. Then you can do a better selling job because you know more than you did when you started.

Listen during meetings, too. This is one of the best times to pick up sales points and find disagreement between otherwise agreeable allies.

Listen to the words and to the tone. You'll be able to tell who is leading whom. You can't learn without listening, and the more you know, the better your chance of obtaining your goal in the meeting.

Don't let your mind wander or focus on objections, and don't spend your pre-selling time trying to develop responses instead of concentrating on what has been said.

Listen, listen, listen . . . there is no substitute for listening. Especially during the pre-sell period.

Listening is one of the meeting skills everyone can perfect. If you become a better listener, your pre-selling will improve. And in addition, your reputation as a masterful meeter will be well launched.

4 | Defining the Agenda

The agenda is one of the two most powerful tools in meeting management. The other—minutes of the meeting—is covered in Chapter 10.

Weeks before two heads of state meet, aides from both sides begin arguing over the agenda. The meeting will be limited to discussing those issues.

In business, the agenda serves the same purpose. It focuses discussion on certain matters. Except in the most formal business conferences, though, the agenda isn't quite as limiting as it is when heads of state confer.

FOCUS

Think of the agenda as a device to focus your meeting. A meeting with no agenda will have no focus and the results will be fuzzy. Too many side issues slip into consideration and, finally, like the famous Caucus Race witnessed by Alice in her Wonderland dream, all the attendees end up chasing each other around in circles.

Focus, not domination. The purpose of an agenda is to center or direct the attention of those in the meeting to the reason for the meeting. It limits discussion; issues not pertaining to those on the agenda shouldn't come up. If they do, the meeting leader should use the agenda to end discussion of superfluous matters.

AN AGENDA FOR EVERY MEETING

Agendas can be formal, informal, or anywhere between. They can be complex or quite simple, short or awfully long, specific or general. The operative rule is: If there is a meeting, there ought to be an agenda.

Many managers seem to feel the agenda is a nuisance. If everyone knows why a meeting is being called, they reason, why bother putting it on paper? It is one more memo in a world already too full of memos.

The answer to this is easy. In a sense, an agenda is a written promise from the person calling a meeting to those attending. By defining what is to be discussed, the leader helps clarify thinking about what the meeting should accomplish. More, it is a commitment from the person calling the meeting to limit discussion to the matters on the agenda, which allows attendees to prepare themselves to discuss those matters. This makes for effective meetings, because most of those attending will have the background to deal with the issues under discussion. Notice the word "most" attending. One sad but true fact: There are few meetings in which everyone is prepared. Usually, it's the same person, over and over. This seems to be something business management has to tolerate.

Keep in mind that an agenda is a promise from the meeting leadership to the attendees. It will help you define the contents of a good agenda.

YOUR PERSONAL AGENDA

Remember the Meeting Mandate: Know what you want from a meeting before you attend. This rule forces you to have a personal agenda, as well as a public one. In fact, many top executives handwrite their personal agenda for the meeting on the "official" agenda, so they can refer to it during a conference.

Your personal agenda for the meeting should match and complement the issued agenda, or you will be the source of disruptive comments which lead the discussion astray. Don't be a disrupter, be a contributor.

Your personal agenda for a meeting can be a step-by-step outline of how you wish to proceed toward your goal. Your personal agenda can include tactics you've developed to deal with the opposition. It doesn't have to be in writing, as long as you can keep it in mind. Writing it serves as a reminder during heated debate. Your personal agenda is your meeting guide and, properly constructed, will raise a meeting's productivity.

Good management, when evaluating meeting performance, often ignores who won or who lost arguments and remembers those who made the meeting a valuable experience instead of a waste of time.

AGENDA CONTROL

This is almost too obvious, but just in case everyone hasn't gotten the point, agenda control equates to meeting control. Not meeting-domination, maybe, but surely control.

Building an agenda means extra work. No effective manager needs more work. So the agenda can become a litmus test. If the meeting and your meeting goal are important enough to cause you to take on more work so it will be easier to obtain your goal, then volunteer to prepare the agenda. For the extra effort, you will bring yourself closer to your goal-attainment.

If you can limit the topics to be discussed, you allow more time for topics vital to your cause. If you can limit the number of items under consideration, you can expect attendees to be more informed about each of those items. Which means more knowledgeable contributions from attendees. If you can limit time for discussion of some items, you can give those items you consider important extra minutes for debate.

If you see, from pre-selling the opposition, that the correct moment for espousing your point of view has not arrived, you can orient the meeting in another direction through the agenda.

SIMPLE AGENDAS

Three people are going to meet to bring a new procedure on-line. It is only going to be a 20-minute conversation, but the outcome, concerning steps to be taken, who will do what work, and maybe even who takes credit or gets blamed by upper management if the new procedure isn't effective, is important, both to the managers involved and their organization. This gathering is important enough to merit an agenda.

The memo calling the meeting, setting date, time, and place should order the points of discussion. Items to be covered first should be those requiring the most consideration. Take care of the difficult business and the easy items will fall into place quickly.

There is a tendency to deal with smaller or simpler matters first, because they are least controversial and require shorter debate. The same inclination is true when dealing with similar points of view versus divergent points of view. Generally, it is better to handle the largest or most difficult items first. So they should appear first on the agenda.

Be sure to head the agenda portion as such, as shown in this example.

To: Mike and Bob

Fm: Jan

Re: Meeting to assign responsibility for our new procedure.

Looks like it's time to act. Let's meet on Thursday, November 3rd, at 10:00 A.M., in Mike's office.

Agenda:
Assignment of responsibilities.
Reporting to management.
Changeover date.
Necessary paperwork.

See you Thursday,

Jan

Once the agenda is on paper, chances are no one will argue with it, and those present will probably follow it.

This written agenda is simple and will improve productivity. Once more, be as causal as your organization's style will allow. Formality can make this simple aid sound like a legal document. And that is guaranteed to cause resistance by engendering suspicion.

There are meetings so small a written agenda is inappropriate. For these sessions, try to use the first few minutes of conversation to agree on an agenda. Knowing what is to be covered and the discussion's starting point will save time and bring better response.

LENGTHY AGENDAS

There is no substitute for a formal agenda to direct larger meetings. When 10 or 12 managers convene, they should do so with an agenda in front of each person. Attendees should have a copy of the agenda several days before the gathering.

Agendas for larger meetings need to be a separate document from the memo which calls the conference. Both are needed because an agenda may be updated several times. It is also a good idea, for the same reason, to number the original and successive revisions. Here is an easy form for a formal agenda:

MEETING AGENDA   Draft #1   November 1, 1990

To Attend: James Francis, Richard Wagner, Lou Frazier,
            Barbara Hearn, Len Thomas, Virginia Made,
            Jack Putter, Sara Connors, Tom Conlin, Leslie
            Greer, Tyrone Moses, and Lawrence Wills.

Date: November 9, 1990

Time: 7:30 A.M. Place: Main Boardroom, 2nd floor of
            Accounting

Subject: Decision on New Branch Office in Memphis, TN

Order of Business:

1. Minutes of last meeting.   5 min.

2. Opening statement by Richard Wagner on
    the Rush matter.   10 min.

3. Report from Leslie Greer on legal status.   10 min.

4. Report from Len Thomas on real estate costs.   10 min.

5. Discussion.   20 min.

6. Decision and assignment of responsibility to
    write memo to management.   10 min.

7. Adjourn.

For alterations to this agenda, please contact:

Barbara Hearn.

A few salient points:

❚ *Confirm the latest agenda.* As mentioned, the agenda is numbered and dated. When reconfirming attendance by telephone, the person responsible for this task needs to verify that each attendee has the latest agenda. This avoids confusion and is one more way of assuring that those who have an active presentation role understand their parts.

❚ *List attendee names.* List the name of *every* attendee. If the meeting is less formal, use first names only. A little more formality is not out of place in this type of agenda, but informality still produces a more relaxed air. Your organization has its own standards in this regard. Abide by them.

❚ *Confirm meeting attendance.* Repeat date, time, and place. It is one more impression.

❚ *Open slowly.* When possible, start the meeting by reading minutes of your previous conference. This delays actual discussion, gives latecomers a chance to arrive and settle in, and allows you to focus on the reason why you are there, and the goal or goals you hope to achieve.

❚ *Monitor time limits.* This helps those presenting and alerts attendees as to how long the meeting will last.

When making this kind of agenda, it is necessary to talk with all presenters, to find out how much time is needed for each portion of the program. The agenda-maker then plans the meeting, allowing what he or she feels is ample time for discussion and final decision making. Putting a time limit on discussion prevents endless repetition of opinions or facts.

If the total time on the agenda exceeds the allotted time for the meeting, it will be necessary to refer back to the presenters and have them reduce their portions of the program. Generally, it is better to shorten presentation time than discussion or decision time.

If the meeting is short, leave it that way. It will grow enough of its own accord.

If approval of the agenda is required, obtain it. Expect some objections and be ready to work out problems through negotiation.

Once the agenda is formed and agreed to by all involved in the meeting, the group leader must stick with the allotted order and times. Exceptions always seem to arise. Set them aside and stay with the agenda, even if it means calling another meeting. It will be more productive, and fellow managers will begin to respect your adherence to the agenda.

The subject of the meeting should be stated as a goal. If the group is to hear information about a project, and make no decision, the goal would be: "To hear and evaluate information concerning . . ."

The agenda should state the subject under consideration in such a way as to be neutral but demand some specific action, such as making a decision, evaluating, and so on. In the sample agenda, under subject heading, a more commonly seen statement would be: "Discussion of new branch office in Memphis, TN." Some of the individuals asked to the meeting might not attend to hear just another discussion. The indicated decision-making nature of the gathering is a far greater attendance spur.

The goal statement also brings everyone to the conference with expectations of action. Not only will managers be more likely to attend, they will come prepared and in a mood to settle issues and make decisions.

SECRET AGENDAS

Secret agendas are seldom found in written form. Usually, two or more attendees agree to bring a matter before the group. They select one portion of the written agenda, say a presentation which one of them is to make, and fashion the presentation to touch upon the matter they wish to discuss.

When the first conspirator, presenting, opens the issue, the second instantly asks a question or otherwise involves another attendee in discussing the secret agenda subject.

It takes a skillful leader to halt this process before the original agenda is destroyed and valuable meeting time is spent on the business brought into discussion by the secret agenda. Firmness and fast action are allies in stopping meeting maneuvering. As soon as it becomes apparent there is a secret or hidden agenda, the group leader must step in, offer to reconvene to discuss that matter (or dismiss it out of hand, whichever is appropriate), and bring the meeting back to the formal agenda. Hesitation to act against a hidden agenda will result in loss of meeting control.

Hidden agendas may be used to delay decision making, force the direction of a discussion, air grievances, and so on. When you see a secret agenda at work, beware. It is a wasteful way to make a point. If you, for some reason, side with the secret agenda-makers, be careful. All too often the use of a secret agenda makes secret enemies. No one needs that.

COMMON AGENDA FAULTS

One of the most common agenda faults is listing the meeting topic in a passive rather than an action/goal-oriented statement. This has just been discussed.

There are a few other typical agenda faults worth noting:

1. *Omit additional information.* The agenda is not a fact sheet. If necessary data must be passed along, do it on a separate page. Keep the agenda just that—a guide to the meeting.

2. *Avoid position statements.* The agenda is not for editorializing. List subjects, presenters, presentation, and so on, by clear titles. It was a fad, for a while, to try for humor in listing activities on an agenda. Mercifully, this practice has waned. If you have humorists in your group, do not encourage them. Likewise, do not, directly or through encouragement, present a viewpoint, no matter how valid, in any of the activity descriptions. This kills attendance and initiative by making the meeting appear to be slanted in one direction or another. Railroads are fine for carrying freight but people object to being railroaded into an action or commitment.

3. *Distribute equitably.* Distribute the agenda fairly. That is, make it available to all attendees at the same time on the same day. Favoring one or another faction by giving advance notice of the agenda or restraining a group by withholding the agenda until near meeting time are obviously unfair practices. If a manager has the organization's best interest at heart, he or she will see to it, within his or her power, that rational discussion is held about controversial matters. Agenda favoritism clouds the openness and honesty of a meeting.

LAST-MINUTE AGENDA CHANGES

Last-minute changes in the agenda should be avoided. At times, as when a presenter is ill and the meeting is held on schedule, changes are necessary. But most just-before-the-meeting alterations are done with malice aforethought in an effort to control the conference.

Some changes don't look harmful. Mary, scheduled as one of the speakers, calls and says, "I've talked to Fred. He has more experience in this area than I do, so he's agreed to make the presentation." Sounds logical, only it is odd happening two hours before the meeting. Mary has known about her position on the agenda for a week. Now she suddenly decides someone else is better qualified? Maybe. And maybe someone has talked her into giving her spot to Fred who is part of a group opposed to the proposition under discussion.

When last-minute agenda changes are suggested, there is usually a reason. Be sure the reason isn't one which will wreck the effectiveness of the meeting. If you suspect this to be the case, have a rational discussion with those trying to engineer the changes, basing your position on the published agenda which has been accepted by those who will attend.

If changes are insisted upon, take the floor as soon as the group has been called to order and announce the proposed change, making it clear who proposed the alteration. If there is discussion or resistance, let those who wish the changes explain. Do not be put in the position of running interference for them, or it will appear you are leagued with their faction.

If a legitimate last-minute change is necessary, try to inform everyone who will attend before they gather. If this is impossible, have corrected agendas, showing the substitution, ready to hand out as soon as each person arrives. Then open the meeting by verbally stating the reason for the change.

If it is your duty to control the agenda, make every effort to be fair-minded, and give the impression of impartiality.

FILING AGENDA SHEETS

No one needs to keep more paper. Even so, if you are serving on a regularly convened committee or on a special task force which will meet frequently for several weeks, the agenda sheets have another use.

Make margin notes concerning the presenters. Time their presentations, to see if they run long, and listen, to define their position. Keep the sheet for reference.

The agenda then becomes a capsuled history of the meetings, which can be useful. Checking through several sessions, it is possible to detect individual positions on issues as they strengthen or switch entirely.

Don't save all agendas, just the ones which deal with long-term assignments. Properly noted, they can be an excellent source for gaining understanding of your fellow committee members.

SUMMARY

The agenda is a powerful meeting tool. Control of the agenda provides a direct control of the conduct, if not the outcome, of a meeting. Agendas can be simple and casual or detailed and formal. Agendas should contain a goal-oriented statement of purpose for the meeting.

Avoid common agenda faults. Don't try for humor, don't use the agenda as a means of disbursing facts, don't editorialize, and do your best to see to fair distribution of the document.

Be leery of unnecessary last-minute agenda changes. And use your agenda sheet to record the proceedings if the group is going to have a long-term relationship.

You now know more about agendas than most experienced businesspeople. Use your knowledge wisely.

5 | Basic Meeting Skills

The beginning of every meeting is important to the success of the meeting. An adage holds that "Well begun is half done." When applied to meetings, there is a great deal of truth in that old saw.

Well-run meetings are similar to well-written plays, they have a definite beginning, middle, and end. Let's begin at the beginning.

CONVENING THE MEETING

When a group gathers in a room, a conversational mingling takes place as acquaintances greet one another, exchanging pleasantries. This is productive, psychologists say, because it relaxes everyone and helps re-establish relationships which may later, in the heat of discussion, become strained.

Use this time to associate names with faces you do not know, speak to allies, and be friendly to those you suspect will oppose your views. The latter is important because you want managers with conflicting stances to understand there is nothing personal in your position. You are dealing with issues, not personalities. It is especially vital when serving on long-standing committees, where you will find yourself allied with and aligned against the same individuals over and over again.

This informal period is actually part of the meeting. Managers tend to feel the meeting begins when the chair calls order. This is not so. The meeting begins when you enter the room.

Use part of this time to check the agenda with the chairperson, to catch last minute changes before you are caught offguard. If you are in charge of the agenda and there have been last minute changes, be sure, through informal contacts, that everyone is aware of the alterations.

If you are chairing the meeting, study the group to be certain everyone has met everyone else. If strangers are present—a trio of consultants, for example, who have come to make a presentation—see that they are introduced to the group individually before the formal meeting begins. Try to identify anyone you don't know.

Personally introduce visitors to individuals in your group so there can be casual contact before business is discussed. Don't leave a visitor standing alone, left out of the general conversation. Stay with him or her. If you are called away, find a stand-in so introductions between guests and committee members can continue.

Be sure you personally introduce yourself to each stranger. There is no need to chat long; smile, shake hands, and thank the newcomer for attending. Sooner or later, you'll be the outsider at someone else's meeting and glad for a friendly face.

THE CRITICAL LULL

The person in charge of the group should gauge this pre-meeting activity and convene the group when the action falls into the first lull. It is hoped everyone will be present by this time.

There is a natural lull in every preliminary gathering period. The last attendee arrives, greetings are exchanged, some individuals have taken their places at the table, papers are being arranged, and so on. This natural lull, or just before it, is the time to begin. Be aware of that moment. If the group leader misses it and continues chatting, some attendees will become impatient. Try to start every meeting with each person present in the best mood possible.

If the leader misses the lull cue, and you are on good terms, let him or her know it's time to commence. No words need be exchanged. Catch his or her eye, point to your watch, and look at the table. If you have to, mumble a catchword. It is time to act and waiting longer will not have a salutary effect.

In small groups of three or four, the greeting period is, naturally, shorter. Smaller groups will be quicker to focus on business. Be sure, though, there is time for small talk, chitchat, a joke, or other personal exchange among the attendees.

Recent studies indicate meetings are more productive if started after a brief period of social exchanges. This is as true with associates you see daily as with strangers. Only the subjects differ. With a newcomer, try to touch on personal topics: marital status, children, hobbies, mutual acquaintances, and so on. Personal contact will make each of you view the other in a more open fashion.

The lull may come and pass, attendees fidget, and still the meeting doesn't begin. Someone is stalling. Find out why; the usual reason is the absence of one or more key players.

As a general rule, let the lull determine when to start. If the most important people haven't arrived, inform the rest. They will recognize how vital it is to have them present.

Once everyone understands the problem, don't let the meeting stall. Start by reading the agenda. Reading the agenda is a good idea in all cases because:

1. *It involves the attendees.* There is action. Something is happening that holds the attention of those in the room. Everyone present will understand why the leader goes slowly, but at least a start has been made.

2. *It shows courtesy to members present.* Egos are easily bruised. You may have an executive present who ranks at or above the level of the tardy participant, and who may be sensitive about waiting for an equal or a junior. He or she considers his/her time to be valuable. Or, you might have have a superior present who hates to be kept waiting, and by commencing, you save another manager from certain ire.

Be aware that many upper executives have pecking orders, too. If the president of your organization is late and the chairman of the board is kept waiting, there can be stiffness even at that level. It is only made worse by the latecomer offering excuses; "Had to take a call" implies those of equal rank didn't have other pressing matters on their schedules.

If you are a late arrival, enter and take your seat. Don't offer explanations. No one thinks you were goofing off. Best not to be late, though. Late arrivals don't get time before the meeting to mingle and generally are a little flustered when they finally take their places at the table.

Smaller groups don't have this problem. If one of three is missing, the other two can locate the late one, agree to meet later, or do as much as they can by themselves and fill in the tardy one when he or she arrives.

Recognize and welcome any visitors, beginning with the highest ranking executives. Be sure all regular attendees know the name and position of each guest.

Have the minutes read. Opening a discussion of some point covered in the minutes is another delay tactic. Gain approval for the minutes. Make appropriate opening remarks. Minutes and opening can be done in 1 minute or stretched to 15.

A manager arriving late will not have to be briefed on progress of the meeting and can more easily fit into the group. If additional time is still needed, try to start with the least controversial presentation.

BRIEFING LATECOMERS

It is often better to declare an intermission to the meeting than halt a session's progress for briefing a late arrival. Breaking into the session to brief a latecomer can be harmful to the effectiveness of the meeting.

Briefings destroy the flow of the meeting. If the group is working well together, the sudden intrusion of another person, even a regular attendee, can alter the pattern of an exchange.

Briefings, which summarize in one minute what it took the group a half hour to hammer out, give the impression that not much has been accomplished . . . and that which has been done was simple to do. In addition, briefing someone on a discussion in which there are two or more opposing sides, tends to fix each side more rigidly in place as their positions are summarized. This makes negotiation harder.

The meeting leader should be alert to the problems stemming from an interruption of flow and make the decision to recess for five minutes or risk an at-the-table briefing. Each situation must be treated individually but, as a general rule, recess.

OPENING REMARKS

After dispensing with the minutes, the meeting leader should make a brief opening commentary. This one or two minute talk needs to be carefully prepared, because it will establish direction for the meeting. There are several requirements for opening remarks.

∎ *Be positive.* If progress has been made, say so. If the task is quite important, say so. If the job before the group is immense, say so. And add that some of the best minds in the organization have been appointed to the group to help.

∎ *State your purpose.* Clearly restate the purpose of the meeting, as noted on the agenda. Telling everyone present one more time why they are convened may seem repetitious. It probably is, but it is also necessary, because restatement of the meeting's purpose helps maintain direction.

∎ *Summarize progress.* This is especially necessary when dealing with long-term projects. Reminding the group of their progress can inspire greater effort.

∎ *Summarize positions.* Opening remarks should fairly summarize all positions on a subject—the majority's and all minorities'. If position-summation is necessary, a wise leader will clear the position statements with appropriate members of the opposing groups, to be certain the remarks are fair. If you are the leader and don't want to clear those remarks, be sure the facts and your delivery of them are impartial. Imminently impartial. If a leader uses the opening remarks to take a side or to try to influence the group, he or she has probably poisoned the meeting.

∎ *Call for action.* Opening remarks are not a speech. They are a device to prepare and motivate the group. Opening remarks should conclude with a call for action.

∎ *Be concise.* Remember, opening remarks should be brief. Don't ramble.

MAINTAINING DIRECTION

It is the leader's responsibility to do everything in his or her power to maintain the direction of a meeting along the course outlined in the agenda. It is the duty of every attendee at a meeting to do everything to avoid altering the direction of the meeting from the course established by the agenda.

Oh, that this were a perfect world and such would happen. Regrettably, this world is imperfect, so meetings wander and leaders vacillate. Many people act as if the bon mot which just sprang into their mind is the last they will ever conceive, so they must share it immediately. Fun in a meeting is fine, as long as it does not obstruct the flow or alter the direction. A story, humorous or otherwise, which is not in line with the meeting direction and tone, is out of place. Don't lead the group astray. Keep to the issues to be covered. More, help the leader maintain direction.

If the agenda is carefully prepared, the meeting will move towards some point. It will achieve an overall goal. But no agenda is proof against straying.

Individuals who are unprepared to discuss the planned subjects cause some of the damage. In an effort to stay within familiar bounds, they route the discussion away from main topics or onto a tributary of the major issue.

The leader should redirect these individuals gently, but forcefully, back to the proper line of exchange. If the leader doesn't, another attendee should. Guiding isn't easy, sometimes. Especially if you're going to be on the same committee with that individual day after day. One of the best tactics is to say: "John, that's interesting. We ought to look into it further. Now, about . . ." and go back to the central theme. If this doesn't work, try, "Gloria, if you can get us more information on that, I'm sure we'd be interested. On the present matter, I believe . . ."

Two polite tries are enough. Some will not respond until told directly to refocus their attention. There are otherwise intelligent, efficient managers who simply do not seem to be able to keep their thoughts on a single subject. These individuals attend meetings well-prepared and with the best intentions, but stray off onto every odd track possible. If not dealt with promptly, their meanderings cause confusion, impatience, and are horribly distracting.

If you are the leader, be firm and remain patient. You may have to redirect the person 10 times in a single session. If that's the case, do not let this go unnoticed or uncorrected, unless you enjoy seeing a meeting you are chairing become purposeless.

Digressions are introduced gradually into nearly all conversations. As leader, or as an attendee in a meeting, listen carefully. Don't let your mind wander. Pay attention to the discussion. The sooner a digressive trend is noted, the easier it is to correct. Remember the comments on listening? Detection of digression is another reason to pay attention.

Everyone present in every meeting should be concerned with maintaining direction. Each change of course makes your meeting that much less productive.

GROUP BALANCE

In any group, there are varying degrees of shyness. Some participants will sit quietly, never offering a word, while others speak at every opportunity. The quiet types may not contribute much, but they are not distracting. A person who always wishes to talk can be.

As a leader, try to balance your group. If someone hasn't spoken on an issue, ask him or her a direct question. Try to get maximum performance from everyone, which may mean limiting the performance of some.

Be direct with the person who ceaselessly wishes to be heard. "Paul, we've only got 10 more minutes on this. And we need Lou's and Betty's ideas before we decide," is a polite way of urging someone to lower profile. If Lou and Betty, in the example, are two of the shyer members, the statement has secondary benefits because it encourages them to participate.

As an attendee, you can help the leader through difficulties caused by someone who constantly insists on being heard. First, by making sure you are not the offender. Then by recognizing, at the end of your comment, someone other than the vociferous attendee. This can be done by asking a direct question as you complete your statement. Example, "So I believe we ought to act, if the money is available, and since money is Charles's department. Charles?"

This tactic can catch on, and with a little assistance from the leader, the hypercontributor can be fenced into a quieter position.

RAMBLING DISSERTATIONS

In a meeting, each participant should speak openly but concisely. Nonetheless, rambling dissertations are rampant. The same participants tend to do this again and again. What starts as a statement ends up a sermon. The preacher is not the frequent speaker, referred to above, but a separate breed. If the leader fails to act, it is the duty of the other attendees to halt the dissertation by politely asking, "What is your point, Tom?" Try not to be rude. But better slightly brusk than part of an ineffective meeting.

Handling a rambling peer or a peer who refuses to stay focused on the matter at hand is one thing. Handling a high-echelon executive in your organization who wanders aimlessly, is another.

The utmost tact is required; and, sometimes, even that won't be enough. Each attendee has to decide for him or herself whether to make a stand or remain quiet. Most will opt to stay quiet. It's a difficult situation because of the obvious politics involved.

If an executive is known to digress in meetings, the only defense is to try to exclude that executive from meetings you attend . . . this is not an easy task.

It may be possible to select another executive, of equal or preferably higher rank, who is known to be to-the-point and an effective force in meetings. If both individuals can be included in the same conference, the outcome might be a correctional confrontation between them. It is a rather weak technique for handling the rambling boss, but better than doing nothing.

MEETING PHASES

Meetings have beginnings, middles, and ends. The beginning phase has been discussed. It consists of the pre-meeting gathering, formally convening the meeting, review of the agenda, reading of minutes, and the opening statement.

The middle phase is usually longer and is for conducting business at hand. It may begin with a presentation, or attendees can move directly into consideration of issues. In addition to monitoring the meeting, to maintain direction, the leader must participate in the discussion and strive to bring out recommendations.

In meetings, discussion should lead to recommendations. That is the purpose of discussion. Many managers avoid making a recommendation in a meeting because doing so indicates some degree of commitment or because they are afraid their position will be ridiculed. Some fear their recommendations will be discussed and found flawed. Recommendations, in other words, place them in an exposed position. Understanding exactly what a recommendation is, and isn't, helps defuse this resistance to action.

A recommendation is a position taken at a point in time. That position is subject to change with continued discussion. A recommendation is not a fixed position from which there can be no change or negotiation. It is not shameful to make a recommendation, and then, after further consideration, revise or withdraw it entirely.

Recommendations are important because they polarize the group. A recommendation generates agreement or disagreement. It brings discussion to a critical point, so that discussion may become more refined and productive.

Recommendations precede decisions. Recommendations are decisions seeking support and modification by that quest. Recommendations are a gauge of what is being accomplished.

If you are in a meeting for an hour and no one has made a recommendation, you are not in a productive session. An effective leader tries to bring forth recommendations. One technique for drawing out ideas is summarizing. After a statement by an attendee, the leader might say, "I take it you're recommending . . ." The attendee must then either make a recommendation or say otherwise. A similarly effective method uses a question following an attendee's statement as, "So you're recommending . . ?" That also requires a direct answer.

Using either of these ploys, the leader must not appear to be pushing the attendee into a position or acting too swiftly. Fairness is crucial. Attendees should not be afraid of making a recommendation and should expect to have any proposed recommendations altered. Each attendee must understand that the making of recommendations is a driving force which moves the meeting ahead.

POSITIONS

Two or more attendees might merge their recommendations by taking more or less the same position. Unless this group within the group is foolish or ego-driven, their stand will not be immobile.

A position may be for or against a recommendation. It may involve more than one recommendation and be based on a conservative approach to an issue, a radical stance to another position, and so on.

The taking of positions related to a matter under debate signals progress because the debate can switch from less tangible concepts to the recommendations that forge various opinions. When position-taking starts, the meeting is advancing.

A good leader tries to get individual commitment to specific positions. As attendees enlist on one side or another, supporting or deploring a given viewpoint, they indicate their minds have been swayed, and that, of all discussed alternatives, they have selected those they feel are in the best interest of the organization and their careers.

A note: Attendees who select a position on the basis of their career, only, need to be treated with disdain. Those who select on the basis of organizational good, without regard to career, are to be praised, but are a small minority. Considering issues on a personal, as well as organizational, basis is not wrong. This is the route most take.

A meeting is well advanced when position taking occurs. An experienced leader monitors the position taking until most attendees have selected one alternative or another. Then the leader seeks compromise.

COMPROMISE

In attempting to align opposing views, similarities are matched and rejected, leaving only the differences. Some points of disagreement can be eliminated though compromise, as one side gives in to the other's view. What remains, after this process, are the real issues that need to be settled.

Compromise always follows intransigent position taking and is the final act before voting on an issue. An effective leader must watch for the opportunity for compromise, because often it may slip past, lost in a maelstrom of argument.

Compromise takes many forms and is not always offered as such. Each attendee must maintain a position, and at the same time, be alert to compromise, even when it is inadvertently offered.

An example occurs during a discussion in which the cost of borrowing money for a project is blocking the project's approval:

A: So I absolutely cannot agree to this project. Our loan interest is too high.

B: It's the only way we have of getting the money.

A: I don't care.

B: That means we don't do the project. We need to do it.

A: I agree. We do need to. But not on borrowed money. It costs too much.

B: What if there is a way to borrow at a lower rate?

A: I'm interested. How?

Positions that seemed diametrically opposed to one another turn out to be less so. Both concur over the need for the project. Both are willing to borrow the money. The remaining difference is the amount of interest. A compromise in exchanges of this nature can be easy to miss as attendees hear only the advocate of the position they've taken. There is no need to comment again on listening. That point has already been made.

As seen in the example, compromise doesn't always involve giving up a portion of a position. A desire to compromise can lead a discussion in new directions as unconsidered possibilities appear.

When compromise has been achieved, it is time for decision making, which ends the second phase of a meeting.

The mid-portion of a properly run meeting *always* terminates with a decision. Decisions, even in smaller groups, should be made by taking a vote. If that sounds silly when the meeting is among three close associates, think again. It's easy, it's quick, and the minutes of the meeting can show who voted for what.

Expert leaders know when to call for a vote. If you are leading and have any doubt, suggest a vote and gauge reaction. If most of those present haven't framed an action in their minds, there will be immediate resistance.

Whenever possible, if the vote is not unanimous, the leader should try to make it so, by asking those who dissent to change their positions. This often happens and the group is able to present a united front. A unanimous agreement, gained by consent after balloting, should not change the reporting of the original vote in the minutes, showing each person as for or against. The unanimous decision should be recorded separately.

If it is impossible to get complete accord, the leader should act to reunify the group, so that factions developed in one session over one question do not continue into future meetings.

In small groups, you will find reaching agreement among those present is easier and a unanimous decision may often be gained by a personal appeal.

Unanimous agreement is important because such action allows the group to build increasing cohesiveness which will, in the long-term, improve performance. Unanimous agreement also ends deliberation on the matter.

NEGOTIATIONS

To negotiate is to seek a way to blend mutual interests, to discern a base for cooperation, so both sides perceive benefit. Negotiation, then, isn't a hostile act; in fact, hostility stifles negotiations.

In meetings, negotiations are conducted between two or more participants, factions, or groups. Each has a divergent position. Discussion is intended to bring about a mutually agreeable conclusion reached by defining a position which all involved in the bargaining accept as beneficial to a satisfactory degree. That sums up negotiation.

Books have been written about how to negotiate, offering techniques used by successful negotiators, negotiating tricks, clever ideas to use during negotiation, making the other party see a situation from your point of view, and an almost endless array of hints, tips, and advice.

There is only one proper negotiating technique. It stems from an old legal saying; *Truth is the perfect defense.* Truth is the perfect negotiating tactic. If you start from, and stay with, the plain, absolute truth, you will be an effective negotiator.

In negotiations, follow these simple steps, and you will be a "winner." Remember that in negotiations, a winner is not one who gets his or her way to the damage and/or exclusion of other's needs or view points. A winner is one who concludes a negotiation on a friendly note and all negotiating parties feel the result is both reasonable and satisfactory.

1. *State your case.* State your case simply, without undue emotional asides or overtones. If emotion is part of the issue, say so.

2. *Listen.* Listen while others state their cases.

3. *Think.* Don't talk, think. Try to see where the various positions interlace, match, or completely differ. Be alert for semantic nuance, and define words having double meanings. Most attendees cannot sit quietly at a conference table and think. Silence embarrasses them. Don't let silence rush you. Work out your position as it pertains to the other positions and your meeting goal.

4. *List similarities.* When you understand the similarities between positions, if there are any, make an opening statement. This is the beginning of real negotiations. State that you are in agreement with opposing views on several issues. Enumerate them.

5. *Define points of agreement.* If the opposition concurs, nego-tiations may move ahead and focus on the points of disagreement. If the opposition does not concur with your listed points of agreement, then request and listen to explanations, so you can define what you obviously didn't understand. Watch for opposition changes of posi-tion. Variations show their views are not well set and can therefore be altered. Continue this give-and-take until there is concurrence on points of agreement.

Good negotiations almost always start from defining points of agreement. Agreement may be limited to only the basic goal of the negotiation. Even so, if this is accomplished before dredging through points of disagreement, contention is reduced.

6. *Define points of disagreement.* Order the points of disagree-ment, beginning with the least vital to your position. Present your list and come to agreement on the problem areas. Do not try to force an order of discussion at this time. That comes next. Reach a consensus on the points to be negotiated.

7. *Concede a point.* Take the point that concerns you least and open the actual negotiation by giving away all, or as much as you can manage, of that position. For example, three points of disagreement might be (1) the project is going to require extra personnel, (2) the project will be costly, because there will be a cash outlay for new equipment, and (3) no monies are available.

You have defined (1) the extra personnel issue as least vital. So open the negotiation by resolving as much of that single point as possi-ble. Acquiesce to the other side. For instance, "I'll provide three people from my group, full-time for an entire week, to do the research. That's how important I believe this project is. Three people less will be a hardship for everyone on my team, because the work they normally do won't just go away, but I believe we need to act on this. I am sure my people do, too. Three of my team can handle the whole project."

The requirement of extra personnel is a blocking point and you resolve it. Not grudgingly, but positively. You inform the other side that you are willing to sacrifice for your belief in the project. You have, in short, opened the negotiations on a positive, accomplishment-directed note. It is now the other side's obligation to respond. That response will guide your next step.

8. *Seek conciliatory response.* Conciliatory movement must be met with conciliatory response. If this happens, negotiations are pro-ceeding. If this does not occur, proceedings are stalled.

When you immediately concede a point, by accepting an opposing view, solving the problem by offering resources at your disposal, or other means, you establish your tone of negotiation. It is one of reasonableness, not rancor and stubborn resistance. This must be countered in a like manner. If it is, then enormous progress has been made and the points of disagreement reduced.

If your offer is not met by like concession, you must discover the reason. A direct question is the best exploratory technique. For example,

A: Look. I've said I'll handle the personnel.

B: That's not important.

A: Sure it is. I've volunteered to do it.

B: That's not important.

A: Then what is?

B: Money. It's a matter of money.

The true position has been revealed, therefore action must be taken to clearly define that point.

A: Is money the *real* problem, as far as you're concerned?

B: You bet.

A: If we can resolve the money issue, will you support the project?

B: It can't be solved. But if it is, yes.

Further questioning is now in order to tightly define why money is at issue. Is it the need to borrow money? What is the problem with borrowing? Interest rates too high? Lines of credit already stretched? The organization's need for borrowing to sustain quarterly cash flow? Stance against borrowing for capital investment? Precise understanding is required, so proper issues may be addressed.

The negotiation is now on course. In this instance, there may be no way to generate additional funds, so reductions in other programs will have to be considered. Nonetheless, resolution of the money issue will resolve the impasse.

If your offer is not met by like concession and a direct question fails to establish the reason, you are not, in all likelihood, engaged in negotiation. You are in a disagreement, which is an emotional state of mind with little room for give-and-take. Should this be the case, terminate the discussion or move it to a later date, as nothing significant can be accomplished with one party negotiating and the other remaining totally intransigent.

If your offer of conciliation is met by enhanced demands for even greater sacrifice on your part, resist. No pretense of negotiation is being conducted by the other side. It is time to use the "Big T," Truth. For example:

I've tried to show good faith by resolving part of the problem, albeit at the expense of my staff. Now you are asking for more. What are you giving?

No instruction is required on next steps. Either negotiations start, this time with a concession from the other side, or your opposites are not willing to negotiate.

One of the wonders of psychology has to be why so many managers come to a negotiating meeting unwilling to negotiate. It is correct to arrive, as one should to all meetings, knowing what you want. Or even to arrive with unmovable constraints on the least position acceptable to you in the negotiations. (This is not a good idea, however, for reasons discussed later.) But to arrive at a negotiation unwilling to negotiate, is silly. As well as a complete waste of everyone's time.

SET UPPER GOALS, NOT LOWER LIMITS

Go into a negotiation meeting as you would any other session. Know what you want. But do not subscribe to a "downside" or worst-scenario position of what you will accept. Let that worst-scenario situation evolve. You can deal with it at that time. If it is unacceptable, simply request a recess to consider it, then adjust yourself to a new concept of what you want from the meeting or devise a path around the obstacle.

Entering a meeting with an image of the *least* which will be acceptable tends to goad a manager into giving away too much, too early. Set realistic goals for the level of compromise you want, but don't establish lower limits.

One of the typical reasons an earnest conciliatory offer is rebuffed stems from ego. Ego is as deadly and out of place in negotiation meetings as in any other business function. With that said, understand that some cannot avoid ego displays or even ego tantrums. These may be ignited by a conciliatory offer. The ego-driven manager may view such a concession as a sign of weakness and an opportunity to enforce his or her will on the opposite side. Again, this isn't negotiation.

Should you encounter such a response, react calmly. Let your offer stand, only if there is proper response. Remember, it is far better to say absolutely nothing than to engage in recriminations or insults. Silence can make a more powerful statement than the loudest voice.

COMPLEX ISSUES

Many negotiated issues are extremely complex and require an armada of experts and assistants to weigh the impact of an action or suggestion on each facet of an issue to determine the overall effect. This level of negotiation, seen at contract time between management and labor or at governmental levels, is not as complicated as it may appear. The principles of negotiation are exactly the same. Defining positions, in terms of agreements and disagreements, may be more difficult but is still attainable. Much internal discussion may be necessary, as each expert follows an action through each position, to learn its ultimate consequences, but an opening, conciliatory offer can still be found and made. Fortunately, most business and organizational negotiations concern simpler dilemmas.

Enter into all negotiations with an open mind. Know what you want before you begin. Show your willingness to negotiate after you are able to determine similar and dissimilar positions. Avoid emotional reactions. Be cautious of those who press for more concessions from you before making any concessions themselves. Remember that negotiation is a process of balancing mutual interests. And that ego and anger have no place at a bargaining table.

Be truthful. State exactly what you will or will not do. Expect all others present to be as honest and forthright as yourself. And don't be too surprised when you find they are not.

Above all, come to negotiate. If you honestly believe there is no possibility of reconciling positions, then spend your time in a more productive fashion. Don't use it trying to negotiate with those who are intractable, or on that which is non-negotiable.

THREE MID-PHASE DISRUPTERS

In the middle phase of a meeting, three evils can cause untold harm.
The first is ego. It is not bad to have discussions turn into

argument. Unless one or both of the arguers binds his or her ego to the espoused argument.

In a meeting, whose view prevails is not as important as which view prevails. Strong beliefs, based on perception of fact, business knowledge, personal traits, and other considerations, build strong positions. Strong positions build strong discussions, which in turn lead to well thought-through decisions. Strong beliefs, backed solely on egocentric considerations, ignore sound arguments and defeat reason.

Keep your ego out of the conversation as much as you are able. Recognize when someone has his or her ego at risk and do what you are able to relieve the situation. Leaders should be especially sensitive to and watchful for egocentric stands.

If ego comes into play with several attendees, take a break. Time away from the table usually helps to disassociate person and position.

The second mid-phase disrupter is emotion. Some managers use emotions as a weapon, by becoming angry and turning their wrath on those who stand in disagreement to their position.

A manager who becomes emotional during a meeting has allowed a dangerous process to begin. It is self-destructive, because others in the same meeting may use that emotional state to their advantage.

A small amount of emotion in an appeal for action or compromise may lend power to your words. A small amount can show sincerity and concern. Even a small amount, however, must be used carefully, because once the emotional door has been opened, many mangers find it hard to close.

Keep your emotions in check. Be as analytical as possible.

Of all emotions, be most aware of anger. It can be aggravating, in a meeting, to have one's views blocked and blocked again. Some find it upsetting to compromise. Others cannot tolerate a different position or hearing their own position criticized. Anger may be a resulting response.

Try to calm anyone in your group who becomes angry. Often, anger blocks reason, so no attempt to pacify an individual will succeed. If this is the case, recess. Removed from the strained posture, the person may relax.

Anger has no place in a business discussion. Those who become angry are limiting their careers because they have reduced the ability of their mind to respond tellingly with logic.

If you find yourself becoming angry in meetings, and cannot control that anger seek professional help. The sooner such a problem is attacked, the sooner it can be controlled.

Anger precludes negotiation, confuses the situation, and will make even the best-run meeting nonproductive. Anger results in hurt feelings and bruised egos and can split a group which was otherwise cohesive.

The third pitfall is hurt feelings. People have different degrees of sensitivity to the remarks of others. Remember this in the midst of a heated debate.

▮▮ Focus on the topic.

▮▮ Try to avoid any comment which could be taken personally by anyone present.

▮▮ Be especially careful of statements that might be construed to be for or against any religion or race. Does that sound far-fetched? Hypersensitivity in these matters is common and some individuals appear to seek meaning in every remark.

If your feelings are sensitive, make an effort to differentiate between an attack on your position and an attack on you personally. There is a big difference.

If personal remarks begin, help stop them. The leader should act promptly to contain any personal references. Each attendee should assist the leader, both by showing disapproval of such comments and carefully refraining from making them.

TWO "DON'TS"

During discussion in a meeting, don't criticize others positions and don't go for the killing verbal slash which paralyzes your opposition.

Sharing your differing view is productive. Criticizing another person's viewpoint isn't. Work to change that viewpoint, if you like, but there is no need to belittle or berate it.

Indirect criticism is as harmful as the direct variety. A remark such as: "We'd have to be crazy to do that," is an indirect, critical blow at the proposer of the suggestion. Don't belittle another's stance. Win them to yours without demeaning theirs.

Avoid the killing remark which dashes someone's position and his or her ego. Avoid this for two reasons.

First, your own personal safety. If you meet regularly with more or less the same group, and you give into the urge for a killing comment when someone leaves him or herself open, you will make enemies who will be waiting to pounce on you when you provide an opportunity. And rest assured, sooner or later, like everyone else, you will provide that opportunity. Do unto others as you would have them do unto you: a Golden Meeting Rule.

The strongest reason for avoiding the killer remark is the death of one of the contributors in your meeting. Few people can regain enough composure to be productive after being scalded by words that show them or their position to be poorly founded.

Even if a remark is humorous, it can be just as deadly. The killing remark has been with us for a long time. In the 1700s, the Earl of Sandwich, during a tense debate in the English Parliament, told John Wilkes, who was known for his acerbic tongue, "'Pon my honor, Wilkes, I don't know if you'll die on the gallows, or of the pox." To which the non-plused Wilkes replied, "That must depend, my Lord, upon whether I first embrace your principles, or your Lordship's mistress."

Many managers have minds as quick with a quip as Wilkes but realize a business meeting is not the place to exercise their ability.

Don't go for the kill, even when someone with an opposing view gives you an outstanding opportunity. The momentary satisfaction isn't worth lost productivity or the long-term harm you may do yourself.

REPETITION

Repetition is the name given to an interesting and useful phenomenon that occurs in practically every meeting where courses of action are being formulated. It happens in conversation, too.

The group has worked out several concepts. Suddenly, there are no new ideas being offered. Instead, each person is picking some portion of what has already been contributed and is recounting it in other words. They are restating that which has been stated in the meeting, using different terms. Repetition has set in.

Repetition is an indication, to the group leader as well as attendees, that the direction which the group has taken has been thoroughly examined. Now it is time for defining solutions based on a different set of constraints. Repetition can be used to indicate when a given train of thought has been taken by the group as far as it is able, at that time.

Some repetition, at the right moment, is beneficial to the creative function of a group. However, continued repetition is a deadend to the creativity used to develop a series of related concepts.

Example: A group is meeting to solve problems concerning the delivery time of a product. One line of discussion concerns production volume. The group has developed this possibility, worked out the benefits, and it is clearly one solution or part of a more complex solution.

John says, ". . . so higher output means more product in the pipeline. And more product means lower manufacturing costs."

There are several more minutes of discussion, then Joan says, ". . . and we'll realize more profit per unit because of lower manufacturing expense, and we'll have a larger inventory to ensure more prompt delivery because of improved in-stock conditions." Repetition is beginning.

A leader must watch for recapping. When it happens, the group's originality and productivity, along that one channel of thought, has momentarily ended. To continue with the development of new ideas, another approach must be found. The original theme may be reintroduced during the same session, after several minutes, and new thoughts will begin to develop again.

It is the leader's job to direct the attention of the group from the fully explored line of reason into another yet-to-be-examined area.

Going back to the example, the leader might say, after Joan's remarks, "Right. Well, improved productivity is one answer. What happens if we also bring on a new shipping center? To cut inventory time-in-transit?"

The leader has led the team away from repetition to discussion of another facet of the dilemma. Repetition is the marker that it is time to turn to a new subject.

Repetition is beneficial, because it is a clear indicator that the group has extended itself as far as it is able in one direction and needs a new direction to be more effective.

A leader may elect to end discussion when repetition begins, moving the group into positions preparatory to closing the mid-phase of the meeting. Time is one consideration in doing this.

It takes several minutes, after repetition has begun, to draw everyone away from the first direction, which has now become familiar, into the unfamiliar, next approach. It requires even more time to begin generating fresh ideas because new groundwork must be laid. In the example, the "shipping center" needs to be explained in some detail so everyone shares the same concept of what is being discussed.

It is better, in the second phase, to move towards recommendations, if time does not allow for additional exploration. If this is the case, it is the leader's duty to reflect the limitation of recommendations in the minutes of the meeting and to explore other avenues, through additional meetings, before making a formal proposal to management. By using the time remaining to make decisions along the first line of reasoning, the committee's productivity is maintained. Everyone leaves feeling he or she has accomplished something; that the group has dealt with at least part of the problem and produced a workable solution. They will return to the task with renewed vigor and the leader of the group will be recognized as a person "who gets things done!"

Watch for repetition. Use it when it happens, as a guide to a better, more effective meeting.

ENDING THE MEETING

The third phase of every meeting is the ending. The correct ending means a better beginning when the group reconvenes. If the meeting is a one time occurrence, the proper ending makes everyone feel time was well spent.

If certain things do not happen at the end of a meeting, much which has gone before will be wasted.

1. *Summary of Discussion.* It is important for all attendees to recall the logical steps which resulted in decisions, or the reasons for not making a decision. To do this, the leader, or someone selected by the leader, should briefly review the discussion which led to taking positions. "Briefly" is the operable word. A two-hour discussion can be summarized in three or four minutes.

The summary isn't intended to review who said what, when, but, rather, the main lines of consideration which resulted in recommendations, and the alteration of those recommendations into positions.

The purpose of the summary is not to re-inflame earlier rivalries but to let those in the group who are confused about some point in the process see there was a logical progression of thought and action. This increases group solidarity and effectiveness.

Those not confused about the flow of events benefit from the brief review by recalling their contributions, and how their performance may be improved.

The discussion summary also reminds everyone that the decisions were not casually derived or easily reached.

2. *Summary of Decisions.* It's important to summarize each decision made by the group so it can be accurately fitted into the meeting minutes and to demonstrate the group's ability to reach decisions.

If no decisions were made, this summary should reveal why. If the meeting was held merely to exchange facts, the review should reflect this, and if possible, summarize the facts.

In any case, this summary should not be biased in any way. Conflicts which emerged during the mid-phase of the meeting ought not be refered to at the end. The usefulness of confrontation is over; it is time to make the group cohesive.

3. *Summary of Areas Still Requiring Consideration.* If there are further considerations, the leader should outline them, briefly, and if possible, or necessary, indicate the relationship of these new areas to the matters already decided.

4. *Review of Assignments.* The leader should quickly recount assignments including those mandated by the discussion and the normal minutes and agenda responsibilities.

An individual should be named as the manager charged with accomplishing each task. Deadlines should be agreed upon. Everyone should leave the meeting with a clear idea of next steps and a thorough understanding of what will be required of him or her by what time.

5. *Report of Results.* If no further meetings of the group are necessary, the leader must see to the reporting of results to the proper management and writing the final minutes.

6. *Setting the Next Meeting.* If another meeting is needed, the leader should try to set the time of the meeting, before adjournment. If the group is regularly convened at a set day and time (every Thursday at 10:30 A.M., for instance), the leader should remind everyone of the next session and state where it will be held, even if it is in the same quarters.

BLENDING OF MEETING PHASES

The three phases of a meeting have been treated as separate and distinct units. There is, however, some blurring or running together of the three segments. Think of the beginning, middle, and end as individual parts, because it helps to show your role, either as leader or participant, more clearly. Remember, though, that the edges of the segments may overlap.

RULES OF ORDER

Large gatherings, say 50 or more individuals, are hard to manage. So rules of order have been developed to maintain a productive atmosphere.

Rules of order (*Robert's*, etc.) are more widely employed in civic, charitable, and social meetings than in business gatherings. Certain aspects of these rules have been borrowed or abridged by the business community. The meeting is called to order. There are minutes to be read. Motions can be made. A vote is taken. Most high school graduates are familiar with these practices.

Other portions of these rules of order have been ignored in the business world. Motions for adjournment that take precedence over other motions, the tabling of a matter to delay its discussion, and several similar concepts, are rarely used in business.

A review of *Robert's* or other rules of order can be beneficial for the manager if it is understood that the formality indicated in those guidelines is more observed by omission than commission.

Every now and again, a boardroom lawyer appears, armed with a well-thumbed rules book, determined to show either personal knowledge or personal foolishness, and proceeds to apply the total set of regulations to a business conference. Leader and attendees alike should stop this worthless practice as quickly as it begins.

Many companies have informally developed their own unofficial rules for order or procedure in meetings. As a newcomer to any organization, it is a good idea to watch during your early meetings to see if there is some procedure with which you are not familiar. If there is, ask about it, after the session.

Understand the rules of the game before you play.

TOTAL CONTRIBUTION

One of the most difficult tasks of the leader is to get every participant in a meeting to be exactly that—a participant as opposed to a mere attendee. Getting everyone to contribute was discussed briefly earlier in this chapter but it needs to be re-emphasized.

A group benefits from every mind it draws upon. A group draws upon a mind by having a participant reveal thoughts through words. A participant who won't or can't talk in a meeting isn't contributing.

It's the leader's job to try and get every attendee to participate. It's your job, as a participant, to take part.

A good leader will create an atmosphere which calls for participation. If you are shy or reticent, quell your feelings and enter the discussion. It will be difficult the first time, then easier. Remember, a group needs output from every available mind to reach the best decision. So do your best to contribute.

SUMMARY

Meetings have beginnings, middles, and ends. There is a correct place to end one meeting phase and begin another. Each phase has a purpose and is important. Attendees are responsible for helping the leader. Attendees need to be participants.

Discussion leads to recommendations that produce positions which result, after compromise, in decisions. Several factors retard effective discussion, and it is the responsibility of everyone in the meeting to guard against these intrusions. Everyone must also strive to maintain direction, as stated in the agenda.

Avoid ego bashing, going for the kill, and criticizing others. Watch for signs, such as repetition, that indicate the direction a meeting should take.

To repeat, one more time—don't be an attendee; be a participant.

6 | Leading a Better Meeting

As leader of a group, you are responsible for creating an environment in which discussion leads to recommendations, recommendations develop positions, and compromise between positions brings decision.

You are the person in charge of creating and maintaining conditions in which free discussion flourishes, arguments are quelled, and factions kept temporary.

You are the one designated to get the most from each person; to build the contribution of each participant into a powerful, decision-making force capable of solving problems.

Seen in this light, your task as a leader is a rather awesome responsibility—awesome, perhaps, but not necessarily intimidating.

Just as there are concepts for improving personal participation, there are also proven techniques for building leadership.

FOLKLORE

First, get rid of the burdens from folklore:

■ Leaders may be born, but more are made, through their own desire, concentration, and practice of leadership.

59

▮ Charismatic individuals may be able to emotionally motivate a group. You can, too, regardless of your charisma rating.

▮ Do not believe men make better group leaders than women, because men are more "natural" leaders or for any other reason.

▮ That it takes years to learn how to handle a meeting is claptrap. If you meet regularly, you can become an effective leader in a matter of weeks.

There's more, but the general idea is that superhuman effort is not required to lead an effective meeting.

Face it. Some people are more inclined to lead meetings than others. Emotional need varies from one to another, but inclination does not equate to skill or inate ability. *You* can conduct a productive meeting; *You* can do it well, and your use of techniques to motivate a group will improve with practice.

It's up to you.

Remember that business runs on meetings and businesspeople who can run meetings are rewarded. Careerwise, it is a necessary skill.

PRELIMINARY PREPARATIONS

With folklore out of the way, it's time to sift through experience and generate a short list of pre-meeting preparations.

1. *Know Every Name.* Connect a first name to a face as soon as you can. If your organizational customs call for formality, and everyone is addressed as Mr. or Ms., then know the last name. Note, though, in a regularly convening group, first names are more relaxing, friendlier, and engender broader participation.

Do not be afraid, in a meeting with strangers, to issue name badges. Use the stick-on variety and bring them yourself, along with a bold felt-tip pen.

An equally good idea, and inexpensive, is the use of place cards. Cut an $8\frac{1}{2}$ x 11 inch sheet of paper in half along the 11-inch axis, then fold each half in half to produce an $8\text{-}\frac{1}{2} \times 2\frac{3}{4}$ inch tent card, which will stand by itself. Write a participant's name on both sides and place nameplates on the table. A small square of transparent tape will hold them in place if necessary.

Take up the cards at the end of the meeting and reuse them. Seeing a person's face and name is the easiest way to memorize them.

2. *Be Straightforward.* Be open with the group about your experience as a group leader . . . or lack of same. If you are open and natural, others will respond to you in a like manner. This gets the group off to a friendly start.

Do not apologize for or dwell on your limited experience as a leader. A positive remark: "This is the first group I've chaired since college and I want to do it right," is acceptable. Don't make a point to say it, but if the subject of your experience arises, don't dodge the issue. Use it to establish an open and honest exchange.

3. *Ban Alcohol.* If the group meets at noon or after normal business hours, beware of alcohol. People change behavior enough in even the most congenial group environment. Added personality alterations are not required. And alcohol, even in small amounts, alters personality. If you want the best from everyone and less risk of a nonproductive gathering, rule out booze. What alcohol will add to your meeting, you don't want.

4. *Learn Background.* Learn each person's qualifications. Their resumes can often be acquired through official channels by dealing with your personnel or human resources department. If this isn't practical or isn't done in your organization, take time to visit each person assigned to your group. Don't pry, but do not avoid frank questions to learn something about his or her areas of business knowledge and expertise. A direct question is a good technique. "Barbara, we need someone with a financial background. Does that fit you?" is a nice opening.

Present assignments might also reveal past experience. Use your head. Don't probe obtrusively, but know something about each manager's professional background before the meeting.

If you glean a little personal information from your research, so much the better. Knowing Tom's wife is expecting lets you tell Tom that if he has to leave suddenly, everyone will understand.

Just knowing the marital status of an individual can be a personal link that will transcend the business discussion and make for more relaxed participation.

On long-standing committees, try to learn everyone's birthdate and recognize their birthday. This is good for the whole group and is beneficial to team spirit.

5. *Wait to Judge.* Listen, but make no judgments on hearsay. As leader, you will hear remarks about your committee members. Store them away, the good and the bad, then observe. Don't let someone's poor reputation as a meeting participant create a problem that will only reinforce past behavior. Remember that Bob wasn't, according to the previous leader, well thought of because of his lack of contribution, but do not decide Bob isn't going to contribute in your group until he shows himself disinclined to do so.

Make your own determinations about the people you are leading. Take note of their reputations, but do not let the notoriety of any man or women color your thinking. Let their actions speak.

6. *Face Responsibility.* You are the leader. The success or failure of your group depends, to a great extent, on your actions. Don't blame the participants if they take advantage of avenues you have opened. Don't blame yourself if the group isn't as effective as you would like it to be.

Continue trying to improve, enlist as many as possible in your effort, and move forward. Determine not to quit.

7. *Use Highs and Lows.* If you have never led a major task force, an ongoing committee charged with serious responsibility, or other important group which meets to define action, you are in for a thrill. Like all events in human lives, there are highs and lows. The lows can get pretty low; and every leader in such a situation becomes discouraged. Do not surrender. Work through the lows and use the highs to rise even higher.

If your present leadership assignment is less arduous, use the experience you are gaining to prepare yourself for the tougher assignments. Learn about highs and lows now, to be able to meet them later. Determine not to be discouraged before you start.

If you digest these seven preliminaries and put them into practice, you'll be surprised how much better a start you'll make. And in leading meetings, well begun is indeed half done.

Your Psychological Preparation

1. *Be Prepared.* Be ready to lead. Sounds easy, but for some people, it's hard to do.

The first step in your psychological preparation is exactly that: Be prepared. If your group is to consider a matter of competitive pricing, know about that pricing. If the subject is centered on a manufacturing process, know about that process. Be prepared. Be the best briefed manager in your group. Usually, someone will be job-related to the project, so will know more about it than you could be expected to learn. Know as much as anyone else present.

Be prepared. Do your homework. Know the subject under consideration.

2. *Know the Meeting Process.* The second step in preparation is to understand the meeting process and therefore your role. It's a complex role that changes as the membership of your group alters, to accommodate new personalities. There are a few constraints, though, and they are covered in this book. Use the skills and understanding which has been discussed. Know what you want from the meeting (as a leader, that's more vital than ever), listen, practice the participation tips, and put this material to full use. It has been developed by trial and error over 30 years and will stand you in good stead.

3. *Believe You Can Lead.* The third step in your psychological preparation is to understand that if management didn't believe you were capable of handling the group, you wouldn't be assigned a group to handle. Or if your peers on the committee didn't want you to lead, they wouldn't have elected you leader.

In an organization, leadership, even of the smallest group, is respected. If you have been called upon to lead, someone believes you can do it. You have management support.

4. *Seize Opportunity; Take Responsibility.* The fourth step in your psychological preparation is to see the position of leadership as an opportunity, as opposed to an increase in work load.

Responsibility requires extra effort. Responsible performance is rewarded in every organization. There is a reward for your excellence in leadership—provided you do the extra work needed to perform.

It takes more work and more thought to lead a group than to be a participant. Welcome the required extra effort and determine to do whatever it takes to be a superb group leader.

5. *Aim for Excellence.* The final step is to decide to strive for excellence: excellence in the meetings you chair, excellence in the

reports you write, and excellence in the recommendations that come from your group. Expect excellent contributions from the members of your team, set an example by making your contributions, and individual performance will improve. Your team members will respect you, recognize your effort, and return more to every meeting.

STAGE FRIGHT

The best intended, best informed, best prepared managers can experience stage fright. It is a natural reaction brought about by a desire to do well when under observation by your peers.

The symptoms differ, but perspiration, an unsettling nervousness, increase in heart rate, changes in respiration rate, and even difficulty in speech, are common.

Psychologists indicate there is a connection between stage fright and sense of self-worth. Experience indicates the malaise stems from being driven to perform perfectly. In any case, the problem is not fatal. It disappears, for most, within moments of actually beginning the meeting.

There is no cure for stage fright. Everyone feels it to some degree under certain conditions. Stage fright does not vanish as experience grows. It is always present. Since you can't get rid of stage fright, you have to learn to overcome the problem, and following the steps for psychological preparation will help. If you still find yourself anxious before a meeting try these suggestions.

■ *Keep Busy.* Do not isolate yourself before a meeting. As leader, show your leadership by arriving a little early and making certain the room is prepared.

Activity reduces time for introspection, which drops the stage fright threshold. Talk to your team as they arrive. It is a good time for personal exchanges, this helps them relax and helps you, too.

■ *Be Prepared.* If you know you know the business at hand, stage fright will diminish.

■ *Use Routine.* Begin each meeting the same way. Routine is a good defense against stage fright. Start each meeting with a quick check of the roll. Move on to the agenda and state the purpose of the meeting. As discussed earlier, revewing the agenda is a good starting point for any meeting, because this helps limit discussion to the topics listed. It also battles stage fright by giving you something familiar to do.

Routine confines the first moments of your appearance in the spotlight to familiar duties, and making eye contact with the attendees. It's hard to mess that up no matter how fast your heart is racing.

■ *Take Deep Breaths.* Unobtrusively, take a deep breath and hold it for several seconds. Let the breath out slowly, and begin. Don't hold it until your face turns red, or be obvious about the inhalation-exhalation in some other way. Do it calmly and start in.

Remember: Stage fright disappears almost as soon as activity is underway.

■ *Stop Nervous Activity.* Check yourself for the little strain-reducing movements people make to alleviate tension: A kicking foot or leg, knocking on the table lightly with a hand or clenching a fist, sudden angular movements of the head or stretching of the neck. These are all common. Control telltale actions.

■ *Enjoy Yourself.* Try to have a good time. Remember leading a meeting can be fun. One of the nonobjective rewards is the real joy of working with intelligent individuals in a productive environment. Try to have a good time, so the others in attendance can enjoy the experience, too.

■ *Know What You Want.* Remember about coming to a meeting knowing what you want from that meeting? It helps with stage fright, too. Having a purpose provides a mental focus and this tends to reduce the vague anxiety or nervous build up.

Not everyone is equally affected by stage fright. Some few claim to never have it at all. As a rule, though, everyone gets it at one time or another. Don't worry about it. Move ahead, and the feelings will dissipate.

IMPROVING MEETINGS

Several techniques for handling any meeting have been tested and found to be beneficial. There is no special order to their presentation, but each topic covered can be of significant value and use upon occasion. Some deal with maintaining your leadership position in the minds of the attendees and others relate to the quality of a meeting and improving participation.

▮ *Forcing a Decision.* Some groups are indecisive. Others are decisive on most issues but hold back from decisions on others. From time to time, for various reasons, every group resists making a decision, so the leader must act, by determining if sufficient information has been provided, ample discussion has been conducted, and there are no discernible reasons for not deciding.

A good start, if the leader wants to force the group into making a decision, is a statement- question:

> We've had a lot of good information presented. Does anyone feel he or she needs more data before making a decision?

Pay close attention to those who ask for more input. These are probably the individuals who are keeping the discussion going and are blocking a decision.

Find out what specific information each person needs and do a quick evaluation. Is that information vital to deciding? Or is it merely nice to have? Or is the request for more information covering a deeper difficulty? A leader cannot read minds, but can determine the nature of a problem and deal with it.

If no one wants further information, the above statement-question allows the leader to take the group into a voting activity with natural ease.

> Fine. Then we need to decide. Ann, you've summed up your view. Do it one last time for us.

As soon as Ann starts her summation, the final decision-making progress is underway.

If the need for more information is valid, the course of action is clear. Providing the information will break the block to making a decision.

Another way to move an indecisive group, especially helpful if the leader is convinced sufficient information has been provided or there is resistance to action because of forces beyond the scope of the question-to-be-resolved, makes use of the timed-debate concept.

> We need to proceed. There are several excellent points of view here this morning. Starting with John, let's go around the table

once. Each person has three minutes to sum up his or her position or make remarks. Then we'll have our vote.

The manager called upon to start the table circuit should be one who has espoused a position strongly. He or she is more likely to speak freely. Others, knowing the vote is coming and they must take the floor, will pay more attention.

When forcing a vote, try to make it unanimous after the decision has been reached. Reasons for this, covered earlier, are even more valid after a leader forces a decision.

As leader, do not hesitate to force a decision when you feel there is procrastination. Be leery of requests for more time to debate or more information, if you feel sufficient time has been allotted or adequate information offered. Additional time and information are the two most common excuses for inaction. Use your best judgement, and if you believe there is ample basis for action, gently compel the group to act.

■ *Delaying Decisions.* Occasionally, a group will develop an energy of its own and tend to move hastily. Or a member of a group will use a strong emotional argument to sway attendees toward an action not well-based on fact. Or a faction will gain a majority and press for a decision more favorable to their interests than those of the organization. In any of these cases, and in other instances, it may be necessary for the leader to delay a decision. Or even keep a decision from being made during the meeting.

Tactics to delay or thwart a decision are tricky. Mostly because of the reversal of the leader's normal position of pushing for decisive action. The best delay tactic is blunt honesty, for example:

Jill, you've stated your position very powerfully. It's important none of us is swayed by the intense emotional aspects of this decision. Let's take a short three-minute break and approach this again.

Tom, block voting often results in approval of a decision which is great for the block doing the voting but less so for the organization. Let's try to bring this back to an individual situation.

This discussion is moving very quickly. I'm not sure I followed all your comments, Ray. Tell me again, if you will, just how . . .

All these are excellent delay statements. They are positive, break the flow of action, or otherwise defuse the situation.

Keeping a decision from being made in a given meeting is easier than delaying a decision. The leader merely needs to halt the proceedings prior to a vote and once again be blunt:

> We have a serious problem, Barbara. I don't believe our minutes can show enough discussion on this matter. Let's postpone the vote until our next session. Okay?

If the answer is yes, the decision is stopped. If "no," at least the discussion will now focus on the question of how much discussion is enough, as opposed to taking a vote.

It is not good for a leader to simply end all discussion and tell the group there will be no vote. This act will be viewed as an overly stringent use, or even abuse, of power, which can destroy the productivity of a group for weeks or months.

It is better to have the vote take place, then say:

> I believe there are some other aspects of this matter which still need to be resolved. But the time to bring them up is in our next session. So we'll consider this again, at that time.

This is still a forceful stance with the real possibility of harming the group, but it shows you recognize the seriousness or impropriety of the decision just made and intend to bring it to the agenda for further consideration. This gives time for personal contact of attendees, to seek help.

▮▮ *Excellence Evaluations.* As a meeting progresses, a good leader evaluates the session for excellence of participation and contribution.

One way to evaluate is to imagine how statements will appear in the minutes. Every member of your group will read those minutes, so it is a good method to communicate with them. And in many cases, the minutes are read by upper management, so it is a means of displaying the capabilities and merits of the group you lead. At the same time, you are saying something nice about your own role, too.

Ideas introduced in meetings run from the prosaic or mundane through brilliant insights. Want to guess which class of concepts is most common? That's why excellence, when found, should be recognized. And why the leader should evaluate each session in terms of excellence in contributions, decisions, position, and so on.

Those who are capable of exceptional performance on one occasion are capable of exceptional performance again. Recognition helps motivate them to repeat this activity.

▪ *Leader Participation in Discussion.* Leaders have a tendency to voice opinions or take positions and expect to have their stance given somewhat differential respect. There is also an inclination for attendees to offer this respect to a leader's position or comments.

When a leader enters into discussion or states a position, that leader should mentally relinquish any authority over the body for the time required to make necessary statements, so as to be equal with every other attendee. This can make for problems if the leader switches between being the person in charge to being one of the group and back to the person in charge too many times.

As long as the meeting is progressing at a pace satisfactory to the leader, remaining on target, and good, sound suggestions are being offered, the leader should remain in a nonparticipative position, refrain from comment, and observe.

The exception to nonparticipation occurs when the leader is able to make an outstanding contribution to the session. This should be done. Then he or she should retire into the previous observational position.

A group leader is not supposed to introduce all the ideas or even most of the ideas or even the best ideas. He or she is charged with creating an environment where ideas can flourish and human interaction may generate new and better concepts. That's a tough role. Don't make it tougher by trying to be a full-time participant in the group's discussions. Your contribution is best made in guiding the group and providing creative conditions.

Minimize your discussion participation. Maximize the others' involvement. When you have a sterling idea, state it, then resume your role. The ability to do this makes reputations. "She doesn't say much, but when she comes up with an idea, it's exceptional," is an accolade worth having.

Do your job and let the other participants do theirs. This extends to casting votes. Abstain, unless there is a tie. Then you can decide to participate, by breaking the impasse, or to continue in the leader position, by saying: "We don't seem to be together on this. Let's spend a few more minutes discussing it."

As leader, lead.

▪ *Note Taking.* Good leaders take brief notes as a meeting progresses, to record changing positions and strengthening points of view. Note-taking doesn't have to be copious, but must provide information for on-the-spot recognition ("Ellen made a fine point. Jack, seems to be in disagreement. Why?") of a quality thought, or a strong opposition. It's not necessary to be able to recreate the entire meeting from your notes, but the high spots should be clearly visible.

Let the other attendees know why you are taking notes. Explain that it is your way of keeping up with the discussion and decisions, to be sure to get the exact wording used by the group. If the participants see you scribbling fiercely, they may decide you're not paying attention, working on something else, or giving them some kind of personal score, like a report card. So tell them why you take notes.

Take notes so you can see the turning points in a session and to serve as a check on the minutes, if you are not responsible for them.

Take notes because reference to those notes, over a period of time, will reveal the star performers on your committee or in your group.

Take notes to determine if you need to adjust the time allotted to each of the three meeting phases.

Take notes and the notes will help you become a better leader.

ORDER

A leader must maintain control of the group. At all times? No, at the opening, towards the end of discussion while positions are being taken, and at the end. At other times, he who leads best leads least.

Progress is not made by disorderly groups. The leader is responsible for maintaining order.

Most mature business managers are not rowdy. Nor are they disrespectful of authority. So how does disorder creep into a meeting and become a disruptive force?

There are some natural tendencies. A leader must know these to be able to deal with them as they arise.

1. *Increasing Volume.* Watch a group of people interacting. The volume of noise they produce has a pattern. They begin by talking normally, then one, distracted, says, "What?" to a conversational partner, the partner repeats his or her sentence in a louder tone, and the volume of sound grows, stair-stepping upwards one notch at a time until the group is far noisier than at the beginning. At this point, the sound level will fall to a lesser volume which will be higher than the point of origination, and the the process will begin again.

Four different groups of two or three at a conference table will show this same pattern as they confer in separate committees. The leader must monitor this sound level and keep it low. Most people don't think well in loud, noisy environments. High volumes of sound also make most individuals a little tense and this can cause overreaction to differing views, etc.

2. *Talking While Others Speak.* In a group of 10, there will usually be one or two who cannot resist talking to those sitting on either side while someone has the floor. This muted whispering, which often produces grins, is disturbing to the speaker and vies for the attention of the rest of the group. If you are confronted with a habitual whispering offender, speak to that person in private. If that doesn't work, stop the speaker, correct the problem, and let group pressure work on the individual.

This may sound schoolmasterish, and to the extent every classroom group has the same tendencies, it is. But it is part of the leader's role to maintain order, which means giving every participant an equal opportunity for expressing views and influencing the group.

RECOGNIZING SIMILAR POINTS OF VIEW

Another necessary leader skill is the ability to recognize points of view that are the same but have been expressed differently.

It happens frequently that someone makes a statement, there is discussion, then another person makes a statement with the same meaning as the original comment but couched in different terms. Arguments actually ensue over which statement is correct even though both are essentially the same.

One of the common causes of lack of recognition is jargon, language used by one department or office that is different from the normal language used by the rest of the organization. There is marketing jargon, sales jargon, manufacturing jargon, financial jargon, and so forth.

Watch for jargon-mongers. Do not hesitate to ask for the meaning of a statement you consider unclear or ambiguous because of professional language. It will help communication.

Pay attention to the statements in a discussion and to the positions of the debaters. If they are the same, or nearly so, bring them together.

If another attendee believes two positions are the same except for the way they are stated, give this person the floor. A third-party explanation could stop confusion before it becomes a big enough problem to involve your action.

AVOIDING PROLONGED MEETINGS

Business operates on rigorous schedules, so time is valuable. Don't waste it by prolonging your group's meetings past the point of productivity.

Deadlines give urgency which can help even highly productive meetings become more effective. Let everyone know your meeting has a definite endpoint—a time at which the session is over. Some leaders like to put a time on the agenda. This is a bit restrictive and if the meeting goes over the indicated time too often, there will be a tendency to disregard the agenda because of the inaccuracy.

A preferred solution is to state, during the leader's opening remarks, that several attendees are on tight schedules and must leave at a set hour. Then get directly to business.

During the second phase of the meeting, if discussion is going longer than needed, the leader can then set a revised time limit. "We've got to be out of here by three, group," is a statement that will speed deliberation. This is a good technique even when creativity is high, because an impending deadline brings forth a feeling of immediacy and hastens response.

A leader should allow the natural tendency of the group at each session to exert at least some control over meeting length. Likewise, there will be days when the end of the meeting is apparent to an observant leader, and that leader should act to end the session.

If the group is having a highly creative day and their ideas are not flagging as the time to adjourn approaches, a leader must understand that it is impossible to guarantee recapture of the same spirit once the group leaves. This is an excellent place to break into the discussion, ask if everyone can stay an extra 15 or 20 minutes, get approval, then return the floor to the original speaker. This is a subtle method of inserting a deadline and keeping the group performing.

A leader can then let the meeting continue up to a half hour, if the idea flow demands it, and no one will be upset. These are the meetings which can produce great concepts. Going to the next appointment, even if late, attendees will feel it was a valuable use of their time.

AFTER THE SESSION

A leader's responsibility does not end at adjournment of the meeting. There are a number of responsibilities remaining.

One of these is getting your group back to other duties without an inordinate loss of time. Many managers have a tendency to hang around the meeting room a while, possibly having a final cup of coffee, while talking to other participants. Others bolt and run as soon as adjournment is announced, gathering their belongings in a flurry and striding purposefully away. A brief, after meeting moment, in which informal personal contact can be re-established, is beneficial, especially if the leader can arrange friendly exchanges between those who have been opposed in the session.

It is wise to postpone the rapid exit of anyone who has been involved in heated debate. Make a remark to them, then talk for a moment before letting them go. You're doing that person a favor by allowing an opportunity to relax after the rigors of discussion. He or she will return to duty in a better mood and be more productive.

Be careful not to take sides during informal exchanges after a meeting. What you say, as leader, can be construed as support, not only for the person but for views that individual espouses.

If you congratulate someone for having offered a good idea, be specific, to lessen opportunity for misunderstanding. If you discuss a position with someone, let caution rule your words. Be fair and ready to state there is value in the opposing position, too. Do not get caught in the middle of a controversy you have helped create. It is detrimental to your leadership position to be pulled into an argument or be seen as siding with one faction against another.

Remember, spirits can run rather high after a fast-paced session. It takes most people time to relax and review. Positions immediately after a meeting are still influenced by the discussion during the meeting. Rehashing those positions informally only slows the process of disassociated review by making the positions stronger in an individual's mind. When you are circulating after a session, watch for this. If you see two or three attendees still bolstering each other's mutual position, insert yourself into the group. Your presence may quell their discussion.

Don't let lingerers linger too long.

At meeting end, your goals are to make the necessary level of personal contacts, heal any open wounds caused by the discussion or decision, and get your team back to their other tasks without undue waste of time. That's a full schedule.

DEALING WITH PERSONALITY CONFLICTS

The leader of any group, large or small, has a tough task. It is a stressful job. At times, you will feel the very participants you are trying to serve are fighting you.

Don't be discouraged. Don't be blind to your faults, either. If conflict persists between you and one of your committee members, it must be settled. Straight talk will do it most of the time. When it won't, you are probably confronting a conflict of personalities.

These exist. They are natural, caused by the normal reaction of one person to another. It's almost like love at first sight—only it's not love that's involved.

A personality conflict must be resolved or your group will be split. The dislike the individual shows for you is probably equal to the disdain you feel. (That's a real clue about the basis of your problem. Mutual disdain, rapidly developing from first contact and going unrelentingly onward toward dislike and finally near-hate, is almost always due to personality conflict.)

The basis of the difficulty is emotional, so there is no logical "cure." The emotional cause precludes rational behavior, probably from either person involved, and such emotionalism seeks support, thus creating factions. No leader can withstand a split long.

The solution is to remove the individual with whom you have the conflict and replace him or her. It's unfortunate, sometimes, because you may be losing an able person. That's the way it is, however, and procrastination only compounds the difficulty of the situation and the damage caused.

Be sure, before you act that the individual isn't merely a very vocal person and is actually expressing the true feelings of your group to your face. Be brutal in your analysis. Ask other members of the group, if necessary. If you discover the problem is you, try to resolve it. If the problem is another person engaged in a personality conflict with you, you must act.

HANDLING A HOSTILE GROUP

More than one executive and manager has found him or herself in charge of a group that has been together for some time. As a newcomer, it is easy to inadvertently break traditions and create animosity. In fact, in this situation, it would be hard not to.

Do not try to be the same personality as the individual you

replace. Be yourself. Get other participants to be themselves. Tell the group what you want to accomplish, and if possible, compliment them on aspects of their past performance. Refer to the previous meeting leader only once, but *do not* acknowledge that you "have some big shoes to fill" or make other comparison remarks. Tell the group sincerely that you are proud of your new association with them, and then get down to business.

The best transition technique is to produce successes and give everyone the feeling he or she has been a contributor to that success. Start off striving for excellence and don't look back.

REJUVENATING YOUR LEADERSHIP SPIRIT

Sooner or later, every group leader who tries hard becomes discouraged. Sooner or later, no matter what you may do, the spirit of leadership dwindles.

Watch for flagging spirits. Telltale signs are dull meetings, listless performance by attendees, fractionating, and lack of direction. Prevent boredom by periodically reviewing achievements and setting new goals. A new goal is spirit wax. It makes your leadership spirit shine brighter. Don't be discouraged.

ENDING MEETINGS

After meeting activities and the importance of personal contact have been discussed earlier. The actual end of a meeting's third and final phase deserves additional comment.

What is done in the final few minutes of the regular meeting, after the last vote has been taken, the closing summation delivered in a positive fashion, and all business is completed, sets up following sessions.

Here is a brief checklist, with discussion where required. Use the following suggestions and you'll end properly.

1. *Final Summation.* Summing up is your opportunity to point out positive results, make attendees feel good about their contributions and look forward to the next session. This is important; make it short but upbeat and positive.

2. *Work Assignments.* Each participant must have a clear understanding of what he or she is required to do before the group

reconvenes. Run through assignments, one at a time, using names. The fastest way to do this is by reading a list. Call on each participant and have him or her relate required tasks. This way, the leader can see that each person has a clear picture of work to be done.

If the meeting runs long, there is a tendency to skip over this task of reading assignments. Resist the temptation. If someone has to leave the meeting early, or, if because of absolute necessity, this portion of the closing must be dropped, send each attendee a memorandum outlining assignments. Do not rely on the minutes to act as a reminder.

Each participant must leave the session with full and complete understanding of his or her next task. As leader, it is your duty to make sure this happens.

3. *Material for Minutes.* As leader, you may want to take responsibility for the minutes. That's fine for smaller groups, not so great for larger gatherings, (see Chapter 7).

No matter who has the responsibility, be certain the person who will write the minutes has all necessary information, including correct spelling of names, especially those of guests, proper titles where required, and any important numbers that need to be included.

4. *Time and Place of Next Session.* This has been discussed before and should be noted again. The best time to set the next session, if one is required, is at the end of the present session.

5. *Attendance Appeal.* Small group or large, ask everyone to attend the next meeting, and if possible, dangle some bait. If an important executive in your organization will be present, say so. That person is a "draw" and can ensure attendance. If there is to be a special presentation, unique guest, or important vote, make the announcement now.

6. *Confidentiality.* If the proceedings of your group are confidential, remind everyone of this fact one final time before adjournment.

7. *Cleaning Up.* Ask all to leave the room as they found it, or better, by dumping ashtrays, discarding cups, stacking china, and so on.

TWO SIMPLE TECHNIQUES FOR IMPROVING MEETINGS

Two simple, little used, nontime-intensive techniques are proven performers in making your meetings more memorable and effective.

Neither has to be practiced consistently. Use either idea at any appropriate time for added post-meeting impact.

TECHNIQUE 1: THE MEETING MEMO

The meeting memo is a personal communication between you and any member (or all) of your group. It is equally useful to leaders and participants alike, although when used by a leader, it can make the next session far more action-oriented.

The meeting memo is not a variation of the minutes. It is not an addition to the minutes. It is a private, positive communication on a specific subject and is an ideal way for a participant to make or reinforce a point.

Meeting memos can be put to many uses, including:

1. *Commenting on Position.* A meeting memo offers a place for editorializing or selling the merits of a position.

2. *Presenting New Viewpoint.* The meeting memo provides a vehicle for the leader to deliver an undiscussed viewpoint on business just conducted.

3. *Preventing Factions.* It may be used by the leader as a tool in halting the growth of factions.

4. *Evaluating Progress.* A meeting memo allows the leader, or any attendee, to evaluate the group's progress in dealing with its business and provides an outlook on the likelihood of success.

5. *Recognizing Individual Performance.* It offers a means of extolling individual performances.

6. *Clarifying Organization's Stance.* It can provide background that relates the problem under consideration to the organization as a whole or integrates a portion of the problem into the full organizational picture.

7. *Urging Action.* It is an excellent device to encourage greater action.

Meeting memos are exactly what their name implies. They are memos that deal with the meeting just concluded. Ideally, they are brief and do not cover more than one or two subjects. Properly used, they lend status to a leader's position.

Here are a few examples:

Memo 1

> Good session yesterday. This project is tough, but if we succeed, we'll free enough money to allow multi-market expansion. Which is vital to our future success.
>
> Bear with it. If our going is hard, it's worth it. Please do your best to help everyone move things along. It's time for decisions.
>
> John.
>
> Next session Monday at 10:00 A.M. Same place. Thanks.

This shows how the group's action integrates into organizational plans and serves a major need. It is a prod to do more, because it's important.

Memo 2

> Sherry did a fantastic job with her staffing proposal. If everyone will pitch in and cover as much as she did, we'll solve this problem.
>
> I know we are all busy, but what we're doing is important.
>
> See you at 10:00 A.M. next Tuesday. If you're one of the scheduled presenters you've got a hard act to follow, after Sherry.
>
> Thanks,

Praise for one person or use of exceptional performance is a spur to others.

Memo 3

> I hate to say this, but we're running around in circles. If we're going to make the progress we need in the time we have left, we've got to forget our inner-company loyalties and work together as a group to get it done.
>
> Please. Stand with the position you think is best for our organization, not just aligned with your department.
>
> I know it's difficult to do this when the final decision directly affects your fellow managers. This one is too big for narrow thinking.
>
> Help us break through the factions which are forming.
>
> Thanks. See you Monday at 11:00 A.M.

These samples show how direct a leader may be in combating a problem or giving encouragement.

The leader can also approach a committee member and have him or her write a meeting memo which makes a desired observation. Then the leader can side with that individual in a second meeting memo supporting that position.

Use meeting memos. They are excellent between-session reminders for your group. Don't be afraid to be direct in these short missives. Sometimes, this is the only way to get difficulties opened for discussion or sufficiently understood so as to allow for correction.

TECHNIQUE 2: THE THANK YOU NOTE

The common thank you note is equally applicable to large or small meetings. It may be handwritten and should be as informal as your organization style will allow.

If you send thank you notes, your meetings will stand out in memory. You must be sincere and *never,* repeat, never, attempt to curry favor by using a thank you note.

Thank you notes may be sent by the group leader or any participant. If you are a participant and wish to send one, only do so if you were honestly impressed by an event.

Here are some examples of situations where thank you notes would be useful:

1. *Excellent Presentation.* A high-ranking executive of your organization makes a presentation on some aspect of a problem you face. If the presentation was exceptional, send a note, thanking the executive for time spent helping your team.

2. *Clarifying Remarks.* A specialist visits long enough to clear up a few technical points. If this was a real contribution to your knowledge, send a note.

3. *Outstanding Work.* Someone on the team does an exceptional job. Send a note if it is deserved.

These are only a few examples. More will occur to you as you consider this technique.

The thank you note must be written. A telephone call, while nice and possibly appreciated, will not have the same impact.

The thank you note is a reminder to the thanked individual that your group exists. It will make it easier to get him or her to come back for another meeting, and on return, be in a cooperative mood.

With thank you notes, be sincere; falseness shows. Use it as an expression of earnest thanks and appreciation for a job well done.

7 | Meeting Minutes

Minutes of a meeting are a contemporaneous history of your activities. Good minutes are valuable. They serve a number of purposes and have uses beyond recording events and decisions.

USES OF MINUTES

Periodic review of minutes of past meetings can reveal a variety of useful information, providing you know what to seek.

If you are a new addition to an established group, minutes can quickly reveal direction of consideration, quality of leadership, and dominant personalities in the group.

If you are the leader, minutes have special value and are, in a way, a report on your leadership abilities.

Here is a review of nine uses of minutes:

1. *Review of Past Activities.* Minutes record past stances and positions taken by individual members of the group. A leader can reflect on these, to discover consistency of attitudes, levels of commitment to various positions, and amenability to reasonable, factual argument as opposed to resistance based on emotional bias.

Combining recall of the actual session with the outcome of that session, in terms of action and decisions made, the leader can judge his or her effectiveness and find areas for improvement.

A newcomer to the group, even without recall of past sessions, will be able to develop some sense of the positions of the most active participants.

2. *Providing Evidence of Factions.* Minutes are a quick way to discover the existence of factions forming within the group and to define positions these sides are taking. Leaders can use this information to defuse the fractionators, and newcomers can be prewarned against these derisive forces. It can also be seen who is leading these factions.

3. *Measuring Group Productivity.* Minutes provide a fine gauge to measure a group's productivity, especially in terms of the number of decisions made. A productive group spends most of its time discussing the issues at hand, not quibbling over past decisions or second guessing management. Minutes show action.

4. *Measuring Participation.* Minutes clearly indicate which, if any, individuals dominate discussion, which individuals tend to have the most influence on the thinking of the other attendees, and which individuals are not actively participating.

5. *Measuring Leadership.* Accurate, detailed minutes are one sign of quality group leadership. Executives use this criteria when evaluating managers. A newcomer to a group will benefit from the use of the same information.

6. *Measuring Management Confidence*. Minutes which show a group has access to confidential information indicate upper-echelon confidence in that group. If confidential information is used on a regular basis, it shows the group is well-run and cohesive. Had information been leaked, the committee would have been denied further access.

7. *Summarizing Proceedings.* Minutes allow each manager in attendance at a session to see a single, cohesive report of what transpired. This strengthens the group and promotes unity.

8. *Recognizing Individuals.* The minutes are an excellent communications tool. Every attendee reads them, as well might top management of an organization. Recognizing individual performance in the minutes can be a real motivator both for the recognized individual as well as those who would like similar recognition.

9. *Giving Insight into the Group.* Orderly minutes are a strong indication of orderly meetings. Informal minutes show an informal meeting style.

There are other revelations in minutes, but the above listing will provide insight into what can be learned and deduced by reviewing them. If you have someone you are considering for promotion, and that individual has led a group or chaired a committee, a review of the minutes could be quite revealing and well worth your time.

WHO PREPARES THE MINUTES

In small groups, preparation of minutes should be the responsibility of the leader. The leader might not actually write the minutes, but is responsible for their content and is the logical person to be in charge of this activity.

In larger groups, someone is generally elected secretary and is responsible for the minutes. The leader, however, cannot just assume this task is being performed correctly. Even if it is, the leader must have input into the minutes at a stage where changes and alterations can be made. There can be no vacillation on this point, and it might require the utmost tact, because it is an intrusion into the secretary's job, but it must be done. The other, equally pressing reason, is that management holds the leader responsible for group productivity. Minutes are an aid to that productivity, are subject to review without warning, and can influence a leader's career.

It is difficult for the leader of a large group to take sufficiently careful notes as a meeting progresses, pay close attention to the assemblage, and exercise the correct amount of control over the meeting environment. Nevertheless, it is better to attempt brief notations than leave the minute note-taking to someone who is sloppy or careless or who exhibits a lack of interest.

If the leader writes the minutes, every effort must be made to be totally impartial, give credit for outstanding actions, and avoid any indication of self-aggrandizement.

Ideally, the leader and secretary should work in unison to produce minutes. The secretary must recognize the various uses for minutes, including building morale of the group, and should acquiesce to any reasonable suggestions from the leader regarding exclusions, inclusions, or wording.

PREPARING MINUTES

There are two primary rules for minute preparation.

1. *Write Minutes as Soon as Possible.* Time edges into memory faster than most people realize. Events which just took place are more clearly in mind than those occurring 24 hours ago. Write minutes as soon as possible after a session.

Do not delay minute preparation. Notes are grand, and the better your notes, the better the minutes you will write. But notes are no substitute for accurate recall plus notes. This is why, in the absence of a manager being assigned to record the minutes, the group leader should either take full responsibility for the task or, immediately, at the beginning of the meeting, assign it to someone.

Recall is important. That's why the minutes should always be done as soon after the session as possible. Not as soon as convenient. As soon as possible.

The minutes should never be written by anyone other than a person in attendance who took notes. Those notes, no matter how copious, passed to someone who was not in attendance, will not produce quality minutes.

2. *State Important Facts Briefly but Thoroughly.* When writing the minutes, be brief but be as thorough as possible. In minutes, the requirement is names and dates and figures.

Many minutes recount each motion and even the major directions and positions in the discussions. Too few tell who forged those directions and who took and/or held those positions.

To say: "Charles Smith moved and Joyce Thompson seconded the motion to . . ." is accurate reporting, and fine as far as it goes. It's also necessary, though, to add information about the discussion using names, dates, facts, and figures, as presented in the various statements.

To be valuable, minutes must be thorough.

A CHECKLIST FOR MINUTES

Here is a checklist for preparing minutes.

1. *Dates.* There should be two dates in the minutes. The first is the date of the meeting. This is usually done as a heading, in this form:

Minutes of the XYZ Committee for the Meeting of March 29, 1990.

Somewhere else in the document, preferably immediately below the title and dateline, or after the signature of the minute's preparer, the date of preparation should be stated:

Prepared March 30, 1990.

Minutes with only one date are incomplete. Users of minutes need to know the date of the meeting being covered and the time which elapsed between that meeting and coverage.

2. *Time.* Time of calling the meeting to order, or time the group convened. If the three managers on a small task force meet at 3:00 P.M., this should be reflected in the minutes. In any case, the time of the meeting is important.

3. *Formality.* The style of writing may be formal or informal and depends upon organizational customs.

4. *Attendees.* The name of each person in attendance should be listed. In case of large groups, citing the names of those absent from the session may be simpler, although with this option, care must be taken not to have this appear as a censure.

5. *Place.* The place of the meeting should be noted.

6. *Body of Minutes.* Generally, the body of the minutes follows this outline: (In more formal style, the wording would change.)

∎ *Call to order*
The meeting was called to order at 8:15 A.M. by Jamie Langston.

∎ *Attendees*
In attendance were: (names and titles).

∎ *Those absent*
Absent were: (names and titles).

∎ *Previous minutes read and approved*
The minutes of the previous session were read. Tom Rogers offered an amendment dealing with item 7, the costs review, and this was accepted. The minutes were approved.

∎ *Agenda and opening*
Jamie reviewed the agenda and made a brief opening statement, which included the following facts: (itemized).

∎ *Discussion: Presentation*
The discussion began with Roger Lowery's presentation of the financial aspects of the situation.

▮ *Discussion: Questions*
Jack Brown and Kate Lee asked several questions, including: (listed).

▮ *Discussion: Responses*
Roger responded to their satisfaction and the group proceeded to discuss the matter.

▮ *Discussion: Facts*
At this point comes coverage of the discussion, including names, positions, and pertinent facts.

▮ *Record of vote*
A vote was taken. The following attendees voted to: (names).

The following attendees voted against that stance and recommended: (names, recommendations).

▮ *Decision*
The matter was decided as follows: (names, positions, decision).

▮ *Call for unanimity*
Jamie Langston summarized the action of the group and requested the decision be made unanimous.

▮ *Record of agreement/disagreement*
The group agreed and the decision is unanimous. (Or, Tom Brown, Quincy Wright, and Steve Pihl disagreed and wish the minutes to show their continued opposition to the decision.)

▮ *Summary*
Jamie recapped the activity and discussion.

▮ *Next meeting*
The group agreed to meet again on February 11, 1990, in the Baxter Conference Room (upstairs, above Accounting), at 9:45 A.M.

At that time, the following individuals will present the indicated reports. Steve Pilh-Financial Resources and Jack Kirt-Manufacturing Potential. A special guest at that meeting will be Hayward Johns, Ex-VP of Finance, to discuss the implications of this issue.

▮ *Adjournment*
The meeting was adjourned at 11:55 A.M.

This is informal in style. Many organizations prefer more formal wording, recounting the names of the individuals who moved and seconded the approval of the minutes from the previous meeting, and so on. It is difficult to understand why formalized, somewhat archaic language has prevailed and, for many, is "the correct way to do minutes." If that is the style of your organization, comply. If you can, however, be informal. It makes the minutes a more readable document.

One final word on formality. Certain meetings, such as those for stockholders, or boards of directors, use formal style minutes and, in many cases, even use *Robert's Rules of Order.* There is no legal reason for this, but it makes the proceedings sound more official and gives them dignity.

Regardless of formal or informal style, make sure your minutes reflect who, by name, did what, including stances on issues, positions on decisions, and so on. Minutes must be complete to be useful.

Pitfalls

The biggest pitfalls in developing a set of minutes are incompleteness and inaccuracy.

Do not concern yourself over the number of pages it takes to thoroughly cover a meeting. Do concern yourself with completeness and objectivity of the coverage.

In groups up to about 15, it is possible to record each manager's position, contribution to the discussion, and final vote. It is also possible to cover the major points of each report presented to the group.

In larger meetings, those with more than 15 attendees, some completeness is lost by necessity, and only the activity of the managers who were key players in that meeting can be covered. (That's another reason why the leader should be involved in the development of the minutes.)

Inaccuracy in minutes is, despite real effort, not uncommon. Be accurate, above all else.

Start by having every person's name spelled properly and by recording each attendee's full, correct, title. Double-check all figures; numbers are sometimes difficult to accurately transcribe. Check them twice, if necessary, but always once with the person who originally presented them.

It is astounding how quickly inaccuracies in minutes are spotted by those involved. Even accidental inaccuracies degrade faith in minutes, so proof the final draft against the original source material, not previous drafts.

DISTRIBUTION

When practical, and this ought to be almost all the time, minutes should be in the hands of attendees shortly after the meeting. Do not wait, as frequently happens, until the next meeting to pass out minutes of the previous conference. Give attendees time to review the minutes. This will make them more effective, earlier in a meeting. If an error is found, correction may be made before or during the presentation of the minutes at the next session.

WHAT NOT TO INCLUDE

Minutes should never contain personal reflections, opinions, insights, or be written from a position. Minutes are factual. Minutes are neutral.

Minutes should never contain deliberate distortion of facts. That sounds obvious, but it is common to find minutes written more for impressing management than functioning as a valuable tool for productive meetings. This achieves little because the performance of the group and its ability to make a sound decision will supplant the group's minutes as a gauge of effectiveness.

8 | Post-Meeting Evaluation

Want a big boost to your career? It's called post-meeting evaluation, and few managers learn to do it. Most upper-echelon executives practice some form of post-meeting evaluation, though, and maybe that's part of the reason they are in the upper echelon.

Post-meeting evaluation is an excellent way to improve your performance as a leader or participant. It doesn't take a lot of time and is guaranteed to produce results.

The key to post-meeting evaluation is to make the process a habit. Obviously, some meetings won't require it, but once the procedure becomes a habit, it will be automatic whenever there is a need.

To perform a post-meeting evaluation, take five minutes as soon as possible after the meeting, grab a note pad, and isolate yourself. Review these three items:

1. *The Meeting.* Did the group make progress? Was the pace of the meeting too fast? Too slow? Just right? Was there a good atmosphere for exchanges of position and information? In general, how did the meeting proceed? Smoothly? In a logical order?

   Make brief notes to yourself. If the meeting went smoothly, at the right pace, and the atmosphere was good, no entry at all might be appropriate. You are seeking problems, not successes.

89

Review the group's decisions and decision-making process. Who stood for and against what positions? Is a pattern developing? If so, why? Did you feel anyone expressed a reason for taking a position that might not be his or her real reason? What other motive could be behind that stance?

Did any problems occur during the session? Were there unusual personality conflicts? (If John usually gets into heated argument with Mary, that conflict would be considered normal. If, in one session, Mary refused to be drawn into an argument with John, or John became argumentative with Paul, generally his supporter, that's worth noting.)

Did you notice any change in interdepartmental conflicts? If so, jot them down. Were there sudden position changes? What caused them? Was it superior reason or emotional reaction? Who made these changes?

Did the group function well as a unit? Or is it faltering? Does everyone have a clear concept of what is to be achieved and a feeling that progress is being made towards that target?

Again, note the exceptions, the irregularities, the anomalies, as opposed to the norm.

2. *Personal Performance.* Appraisals will differ between a leader doing a self-evaluation and a participant assessing personal performance.

▮▮ *Leader.* Let's take the leader's role first. The required notes cover deficiencies, not areas of adequate achievement. Was the meeting atmosphere creative? Was it an environment in which every committee member could contribute? Or was there some problem with the "feeling" of the meeting. Something or someone stifling free exchange and causing dissension? If a problem can be identified, then review what you, as leader did or didn't do to correct the situation. Think of what might have been done.

Was the direction of the meeting maintained? If not, what action could you have taken to restore direction?

Were the presentations of top quality? If not, what can be done to improve them?

Was the meeting dull? Or was it interesting because of the contributions from attendees and their interest in the subject?

Did the group drive sufficiently hard for decisions, or were decisions forced upon them by constraints of time or other forces? Is work needed to guide them in this phase of the meeting?

Finally, sum up and note how you feel you can improve your leadership. Be specific, based on the just-concluded meeting. It's better to note that: "I need to push Joe, Tom, Jack, and Grace. They hold back in the decision process," as opposed to "The group needs to be pushed harder into decision making."

See your problems and potential problems clearly by connecting them, where possible, to individuals. It is easier to consider how to change an individual than it is to reorder abstracts.

∎ *Participant.* As a participant, the process of personal evaluation is similar, but some different questions need to be asked.

Did you play an active role in the session? If not, why not? Were you constrained by others, checked by the leader, unprepared, or what? Answer this question objectively and you'll be able to fix the problem. (Nonparticipation is a serious problem.)

Was your contribution to the meeting valuable? Or did you get emotionally carried away or sidetracked into a parallel discussion, or thwarted by factions, and so on. Was your contribution satisfactory to you? You know how you did. If you encountered problems or difficulties, face them. Note them with care. They probably won't just go away. You'll most likely be called upon to deal with them. Knowing what they are, in advance, is an advantage.

Finally, ask yourself how you can do better—how your contribution can be greater, how you can help the leader, how you can improve both in meeting skills and presentation techniques.

Judging yourself on the basis of a recent past performance can test your spirit. Don't be concerned if the performance under evaluation wasn't adequate, if prior performances have been considerably better. But make note of the areas in which you did not excel. If the same problem keeps arising, don't kid yourself. You've got room for improvement. At least you'll know what to improve.

3. *Fence Mending.* As leader or participant, your actions in a meeting can cause hurt feelings or make divisions. Spend

a minute thinking about this aspect of the meeting. This evaluation should not relate to you or what you did, unless you caused a need to mend fences with those of a different view. Remember: Friends come and go, while enemies accumulate.

Was someone, anyone, offended in the meeting? Why? Was the offense committed deliberately? Or was it inadvertent? Was it obvious, that is, did everyone see it, or only you? Was there a clash between splinter groups? How can their differences be resolved? What can you do to resolve them? Is there a difficulty between the group and the leader? If so, is there something you can do to defuse the situation or lessen tensions? If there is, could you have done it during the just-ended meeting? Was there reason not to act?

Do the men and women in your group receive equal respect and are they treated equally by every participant? Or is there an incipient problem caused by chauvinism or feminism? Can you help?

This stream-of-consciousness laundry listing can be used as a guide to begin your use of post-meeting evaluation. The purpose of this brief period of reflection should now be apparent. You want to form your own assessment of the group and your performance within that group.

Be honest with yourself. No one will ever know what you consider to be your faults or your good points. This is a private matter, performed in solitude.

Your own objective observations are your best guide to self-improvement. Do not be brutal with yourself, but likewise, don't overlook obvious, consistently arising problems.

Make notes. We'll discuss what to do with them in a moment. Focus your notes on problems, so they can be quickly scanned. To improve, you need to do what you do better, and what you don't do so well, better still.

YOUR MEETING FILE

This is a private document. Do not leave it lying around or be careless with it. If you are, it means you haven't been candid enough in your notes or haven't named enough names.

A standard legal or letter-sized folder is an excellent container for your file. Tab it with the name of your group and enter an open date. When the file is closed, take it home. Or at least put it somewhere safe in the office, because it is part of your long-term record of meetings.

Open the file, and on the inside cover, using correct spelling, enter the names of everyone in your group, starting with the leader. If you are the leader, your name comes first. No need to alphabetize here, but if the group is quite large, order might help you find a person more quickly.

Next to the name, enter their exact title. Next to that, list their telephone and/or paging number. You are now able to write or call anyone in your group without having to search for name, title, or telephone. As managers are reassigned or new individuals join your group, you'll have a complete membership history. It may be the only one in existence.

In the folder, clipped together in separate stacks, keep agendas, minutes, your meeting notes, and your post-meeting evaluations, with the most current on top.

Before going to the meeting, you'll be able to quickly refer to your file, update yourself on the planned happenings, and review what you need to do to improve performance. Combine that with knowing what you want before entering the meeting, and you are a formidable, well- prepared leader or attendee.

Meetings tend to generate a number of reports beyond agenda and minutes. Use your judgment, but generally, your meeting file should not include extra information. It makes it too hard to use at the conference table and adds bulk. A separate file for other material is usually a better idea.

Keep your meeting file closed during the session, except for reference when needed. That way no one sees your objective comments of their past activities. Your meeting file is a personal document. Its purpose is to improve your meeting performance by serving as a record of past work, both yours and the group's, and an immediate, during-the-meeting reminder of what you need to watch for or how you can improve.

The meeting file and post-meeting evaluation are proven techniques for improving your meeting ability. They take little time and pay big results.

9 | How to Be a Better Participant

Improving participation in a meeting is a learned skill. Practice and observation train the mind, and in a short while, a manager interested in being a better participant, becomes one.

The two most important actions in improving meeting participation have already been discussed. Here they are again, in a slightly different context.

THE MEETING MANDATE

You'll be a better participant if you know what you want from the meeting. To get what you want requires participation.

LISTEN

The ear is the key to effective communication. Not the mouth. In Chapter 5, the art of creative listening was used to analyze the group's progress. As your ability to listen improves, your value as a participant increases.

PRESENTING YOUR POINT OF VIEW

One excellent way to improve your participation is to improve your presentation—the presentation of your thoughts, recommendations, and positions.

It doesn't take a great voice to be a powerful presenter. It doesn't require a special personality. It does require a mindset, a desire to improve, and the understanding of seven simple, easy-to-master concepts.

1. *Be Positive.* This concept is composed of two parts. One is what you say. The other is how it is said.

   ■ *What you say.* Approach the discussion from a positive point of view. Even if you disagree with another's position, state your disagreement in a positive manner.

   Example: Lon wants the organization to open an on-site baby-sitting service for employees, but is concerned about legal liabilities. You want the service and feel the liability issue, as has been shown in a previous presentation, can be covered by insurance. Lon needs to be reminded of the insurance availability. One tack is to say, "Don't forget the insurance, Lon." A better, positive approach, which doesn't accuse Lon of forgetfulness, is: "Do you think we need more insurance coverage than Jean indicated in her presentation, Lon?"

   Since liability is a concern, Lon will probably answer yes to the question. He has taken a position and your comment allows the group to consider whether or not Jean's plan provides ample coverage. If it does, then Lon's objection is gone. If the plan does not offer sufficient coverage, then the issue becomes tangible. It's a question of how much coverage the group feels is needed, the cost of that coverage, and the impact of that cost on the prices charged by the sitting service.

   Objections to the idea of the service itself are sidetracked because the discussion has grown specific. Opposition may arise again, but not until all present have seen the resolution of Lon's insurance-liability objection.

   The positive statement makes your point, shifts the direction of the discussion to a factual, instead of intellectual or emotional plane, and helps answer the objection of one who opposes an issue which you favor.

   Other examples:

   John: I am dead set against building a new garage.

   Mary: Tell me why, John. So I can understand. Because I know you see some merit in the proposal.

Paul: There is absolutely no evidence to cause me to rethink my position.

Charlie: [Wrong] What about the Bourne study? It seems clear to me.

Charlie: [Right] The Bourne study covers some of the points. Do you think we need more information?

[Note: No effort is made to discredit Paul's position. The focus of the response is on information.]

Paul: Yes. Since there's nothing here, as I've said, to make me reconsider.

Charlie: Let's get specific, Paul. What data do we need?

The positive expression doesn't attack the other person's point of view. It moves the discussion forward by examination of the stated cause of that point of view.

This sounds tricky, but it's not. It is easy to learn. You already know the obvious part of being positive, which is not stating your view in a negative manner.

Example: If you want the group to follow a course of action, you should say: I really believe it's best if we . . ." Do not say: "I'm not sure it's best, but . . . ," or: "If we're smart, we'll," or: "It's our only real option."

Any of the last three statements do not help your position or your reputation as a meeting professional. Yet you'll hear them in session after session, spoken by otherwise effective managers.

∎ *How You Say What You Say.* Part 1 of positive expression is to be positive in your expressions. Part 2 is how you say what you say.

There is a tendency for managers to be tentative in the early phases of a discussion, as they inch their way along, trying to understand issues and determine alignments or sides. We'll discuss one aspect of this later, in Presentation Concept 7 (Take a Position), but part of a positive presentation is a positive voice.

When people are tentative in thought, it usually shows in their voices. Others recognize the tone.

When you say something, say it in a positive voice. Ask questions in a positive voice. This doesn't mean shout or lower your range. It merely means keeping out the tentative or questioning inflection, so listeners will give your remarks more weight.

Psychologists tell us the tone of a speaker's voice imparts a secondary message. Make your secondary message enforce your words, not weaken them. Be sure you speak loud enough to be heard. Don't whisper. Don't yell. You're seeking a balance. You want to be understood yet still have others use a tiny bit of effort to hear every word.

2. *Speak Slowly.* We have many rates of speech. And people talk at individual speech rates. You've known someone who talked so fast he or she was hard to understand.

In a meeting, slow your speech. This doesn't mean ridiculously dragged out so you sound like a recording played back at the wrong rpm. Slow to a point below your normal rate of delivery.

There is tension in a meeting, even as it begins. If the debate warms, tension increases. Tense people talk faster. Nervousness also makes it harder to select the right words, so humans tend to speak more rapidly and less precisely as tension mounts. When you speak, speak slowly, loud enough to be heard, and distinctly enough so each word is clear.

Regulating your speech speed allows you to overcome the effect of tension, adds power to your comments, making them sound more deliberate, and makes it easier for others to listen.

Don't slow you speech by spurting a few quick words, pausing, then spewing another chain of language.

Slow down just slightly on each word, add half-a-heartbeat to your pauses, and say a sentence which would normally take you five seconds to enunciate in six.

You don't want to slow your speech so much that you destroy the pace of your argument or statement. Relax your rate enough to be easy to understand, to let you feel in control of your voice, and give your words weight.

3. *Make Eye Contact.* Watch during the next meeting. In a group of 10, there will almost always be two people who stare at the table or the pad in front of them as they say their piece.

Do not be one of the two. Make eye contact.

Some managers take this too much to heart, and during their presentations, engage in a game of stare-down with each fellow participant, which results in no one hearing their comments.

These individuals would be better off watching the table or pad, because the intensity of their gaze is read as challenge and creates conflict.

Eye contact should be friendly, not hostile; friendly, not challenging; friendly, not sexy; friendly, not intense. Eye contact should be friendly.

When you start to speak, first make eye contact with the group leader, or, if you are answering someone or addressing your comments to another, with that person. Once eye contact is established, move to others, return, move away again, then return. Shifting your eye contact gives the other person and yourself a break, prevents a staring contest, makes it easier not to take your remarks personally, and gives you an opportunity to review the room, judging from facial response, those for and against your position.

A smile helps put your eyes in the right mode of friendliness. Even when disagreeing adamantly (in a positive way, of course), a smile adds to eye contact. (Unless it's a Jack-the-Ripper grimace, snide sneer, or other ugly mouth shape.) Friendly grin, friendly eye contact, and your words are a professional statement of your position, not a personal attack.

Make eye contact when you are silent and don't have the floor, too. With the speaker, of course, and with others at the table, to judge the effect of the speaker's remarks. Eye contact makes some individuals uncomfortable. Learn to recognize which ones are uncomfortable and don't hammer those people to death. Do make occasional friendly contact, though.

4. *Sit Attentively.* Sit in your chair with authority. Even if the meeting is relaxed, sit straight. Not at military attention, but erect. An erect posture gives the appearance of interest. Your appearance at the conference table is defined by how you sit. If you sprawl in your chair or slouch forward, you harm your presentation abilities.

Women tend to sit more attentively, by and large, than men. Most men need improvement in their meeting sitting posture. The goal is to look comfortable, alert, and ready to contribute.

5. *Restrain Arm Motions.* Abnormal arm motions destroy the effectiveness of a presentation. Hand movements are not under consideration. That comes next.

Arm waves look odd at a conference table. The huge, broad, wide range of movements many people use in normal conversation are almost dangerous when performed in the midst of a seated group. Worse, arm wavers tend to be finger pointers at moments of stress, and finger pointing is an accusation.

Check your arm movements. Keep them in bounds, which means keeping them to a minimum.

6. *Use Effective Hand Movements.* Hand gestures add immensely to your presentation. Hand movements lend animation to your words, can help listeners understand your ideas better, and can be used for dramatic effect. Some people do not make many hand gestures. If that's your normal style, refine it a little, to use a hand movement as reinforcement of a good point.

Since hand movements convey emotion, the wrong gestures can make you appear ineffectual or tentative. Be aware of your hand movements for a few meetings, and you'll be able to improve.

Note: This little piece of advice is likely to make a person self-conscious, which affects his or her hand movements. It's possible to be conscious of your hands while you talk. Try it and see for yourself.

7. *Take a Position.* No matter how many times it is said, it's worth saying again. A position taken during the course of a meeting is not one any attendee has to maintain forever. A position can be temporary. It is a transient way-station instead of a death-do-us-part commitment.

Do not be afraid to take a position, then as you develop greater understanding through the discussion, take another.

It would be nice to believe the most skillful meeting people follow the Hollywood-motion-picture mode and remain neutral through a discussion, then, with the wisdom of Solomon (and a script written for heroics) take the right position, fully developed, at the end. That seldom happens.

Managers with meeting skills often take a position at the outset of debate. They base this position on their knowledge and beliefs. They state their position, so others present with differing views can address them and their concerns. They don't take the position adamantly, but do so positively, and with the assurance that if there is ample reason to change they will not be intransigent.

If your experience and beliefs urge you to take a position during the early stages of a conference, do so. Stay with that position until you are persuaded to change. Don't be afraid of position taking, or of position altering, or of outright position changing.

It requires a rather self-possessed individual to simply say: "The position I hold on this isn't right," and accept another view.

Take a position. It's not cast in stone until the vote is cast.

None of these presentation concepts is complicated or difficult. They require a little thought and practice, but time invested in developing and applying these principles to your meeting skills will pay dividends.

HAVING IMPACT

One of the most obvious differences between individuals at a meeting table is impact. One manager makes a statement which is sensible and appropriate. Yet, it doesn't have impact. Another counters, with an equally valid remark, and every person present takes note. That's impact.

Impact is the effectiveness of your presentation. The seven meeting concepts are designed to give more impact to your words.

Recommendations have more impact on a group than conversation or debate. Do not be afraid to make proposal. Don't swamp the meeting with suggestions, but any time you need a little more impact, make a recommendation, as opposed to a statement.

If you don't let your ego intrude, you can gauge the relative impact you have on a group by observation after you've finished speaking. If each person's attention is immediately switched to the next speaker, you've done an average job. If it takes a moment for one or two to refocus thoughts from your stance, you've had impact.

Impact is valuable, but don't trade clarity or calmness to get it.

CHANGING POSITIONS

When you are convinced of a new position, say so. Don't hesitate or delay. You can help the meeting move along by stating your new position clearly. It will help if you also state why you have changed your viewpoint. Others may follow your logic and discover they have missed something during the discussion.

Once you alter position, go forward from that stand. Don't look back toward your previous stance. See all ensuing arguments from this new viewpoint.

The number of perfect positions is sorely limited. Acceptance of a position is usually a compromise, made by selecting the stronger alternative, not looking for faults which obviously exist.

CHANGING SIDES

"Sides" or opposing groups in a meeting are temporary. If they are permanent, that is, one group is always opposed to another, you don't have sides. This is gang warfare.

Sides should be taken based on viewpoint, and any member of any side should have the right to switch sides as his or her viewpoint alters.

You must feel free to change sides. Don't add the emotional weight of loyalty to the already considerable burden of changing position. Business meetings should not be like political gatherings, where there are parties and it is a serious matter to change parties. If there is a sense of blind loyalty in meetings you attend, work with your fellow managers to resolve the problem. Meeting productivity will increase rapidly.

There shouldn't be factions in meetings, but at times they arise, with allegiances built along lines of work specialty. Those involved in sales, for instance, may band together against manufacturing. This is a serious problem and needs resolution if the group is to be effective. Some fractionating is normal, because individuals in each group share common concerns. But when a faction demands loyalty regardless of position correctness, insofar as concerns the best option for the organization as a whole, it has become counterproductive.

Factioning is part of the reason why many upper level executives consider most meetings counterproductive. Management has seen too many decisions made on the basis of what is best for a segment of the organization as opposed to the overall benefit of the company.

ARGUMENT VERSUS DISCUSSION

Avoid argument. Do not be argumentative. If you do argue, stay objective.

Argument and discussion carry somewhat the same definitions in dictionaries, but in business meetings, there is a marked difference.

Discussions dissolve into argument when two or three individuals, each with a fortified position, dominate the meeting and repeat, ad nauseam, their views. None of those involved hears any of the others. Each of those involved presses on regardless, stating and restating his or her position to the exclusion of all other views or comments. The longer this continues, the more fixed each manager becomes as he or she edges close to anger.

Discussion, then, is an exchange of views. Argument is the rigid stating of a position then restating of that position in response to a question, rather than answering the question. When this happens, the meeting has degenerated from discussion to argument.

Avoid arguments. Arguers find solace in others taking their position. Strength, because of the emotional overtones in argument, comes from numbers. The arguer likes to feel he or she represents a group view.

Don't enter into an argument. Don't take sides in an argument. Do try to stop an argument and turn it back into a discussion. The leader should be sensitive to argument and break it off as soon as it begins.

Do not be argumentative. Listen to the other person's view, even if you consider it foolish. Blocking out the view and repeating your stance is the beginning of argument.

Questions require answers, not restatements of position. So answer questions and you'll break your tendency toward argument. If you find yourself involved in an argument, realize that anger is not far away and emotional words can be expected momentarily.

The way to end the argument is to become objective, about the issue as well as the degenerated state into which the discussion has fallen. It takes intestinal fortitude when emotion starts to build, to say: "John, I'm afraid we're arguing, not discussing. I'm sorry. I got so caught up in what I believe, I wasn't even hearing you. Let's take a short break and start again. Okay?"

If you remain objective about the situation, you can stop argument and return to discussion.

EMPHASIZING YOUR POSITION

If every person at a meeting clearly knew everyone else's position and understood why each position was espoused, the meeting would move faster and produce better decisions.

Be certain everyone at the table knows where you stand on an issue. If you are undecided, make sure the others present know that.

Whatever your position, make every effort to express it to each person in the meeting. In a large meeting, where that would be impossible, clearly state your position, even if it is that your are undecided, so there can be no mistake. If your position changes, let all present know that, too.

If a vote is to be taken, explain your position and state why you are voting for or against a proposition. Be concise, but say what you feel.

If you wish to sway others to your position, determine what your views have in common with those expressed and to what degree your views can be modified to bring them closer into alignment with others. Then restate your position in this new light, emphasizing similarities. Re-emphasizing your position as the meeting continues allows others to know your stance. It is a service to the group which you can use to "sell" your viewpoint.

None of the concepts discussed in this chapter are difficult, either to learn or to put into practice. All will help your participation in meetings. Good participation is, fortunately, contagious, as is, unfortunately, poor participation. Set an example as a participant, and others will follow. Even those whose meeting skills do not allow them to contribute will improve as the group improves.

Remember: Every meeting needs the best from every mind upon which it may draw. A nonparticipating mind is not contributing to the meeting and may well be blocking progress.

Don't attend. Participate.

10 | Protecting Confidential Information

The management of every organization restricts access to certain information. This confidential information varies, ranging from personnel reports, to proposals for a new freeway route, to critical operating "numbers" related to the financial statement.

Most organizations, except for the very large ones or those dealing with the government, do not have well defined policies concerning the protection of confidential material. In the near future, because of an ever-increasing access to information, more and more firms will be forced to formalize their procedures or accept loss of confidentiality.

If your organization has procedures for safeguarding classified material and your group requires that data, be certain you follow the practices exactly. It also helps to be aware of and knowledgeable about all aspects of the protection program, as opposed to only those portions which seem to affect your group and meeting.

This chapter discusses certain precautions which should be taken when using classified material in meetings. The comments here are valuable even if your organization has a strict formal policy in secrecy matters. If no such plan exists, the guidelines offered will help control such information before, during, and after the meeting in which it is used.

INFORMATION PROTECTION IS IMPORTANT

If information in your organization has been classified, it was because management did not want that information disseminated outside a certain group. In other words, it has been deemed that material be viewed only by selected managers.

If, even by accident, the material is "leaked" or exposed to unauthorized individuals, problems will ensue. So protection of classified material is vital, to your group and to your own advancement. This is as true for the group leader as the individual participant. Being part of a group that reveals classified material is not beneficial to any member of that group. Even inadvertent leakage, if detected, can be met with harsh consequences.

The disclosure of classified data is also potentially harmful to your organization. There is generally a rather sound reason why management does not wish certain information released.

TECHNIQUES OF HANDLING
CLASSIFIED INFORMATION

Systems for classified material handling have been developed by professionals in this field and perfected over the past hundred years. Mainly, this work was performed at the governmental level. As the need increased for similar controls, business borrowed the techniques and adapted them to a somewhat less restrictive environment.

The first step in the process of limiting access to information is to identify the specific information to be protected and decide how limited that access will be.

In business, three classifications are sufficient for almost every need. Reference to these "levels" of secrecy will be according to their government names—restricted, secret, and top secret. Those in the public sector also classify information according to type, which groups financial data, real estate appraisals, research and development programs, production schedules, and so on.

One production document might be "restricted," while another is "top secret." No matter what the level of classification or the topic category under which it is classified, leaks are possible. But because the number of individuals with access to the material shrinks at each classification stage, so that far fewer managers are able to see top secret documents than restricted matter, leaks in higher classifications are usually more easily detected, and those responsible more easily defined.

Make certain your group understands this. While all material which has been classified must be treated with care, documents in the highest secrecy category will most likely cause greater concern if revealed. So these will receive the greatest amount of checking and investigation after a leak is discovered.

NEED TO KNOW

One of the best techniques for keeping secrets is based on allowing only those who have a need to know access to the classified information. This is a good guideline for any group that deals with this kind of data. And it applies well to the meeting situation.

The leader of a group with access to classified material should ask these questions:

1. *Is there a real need to know?* An organization's secrets should stay classified for the good of the organization. Each time one more person accesses the material, the chances of disclosure are increased. Therefore, the fewer with access, the more secure the secret.

Does the group you lead really need to know? Are you working with principles which would allow the substitution of approximate numbers for meeting purposes and still be functional and correct when the actual, secret numbers are used? If so, there is little or no need to know. Work with the group using approximate figures.

Ask yourself if having the information will make a difference in your group's ability to act.

If you believe the information is needed, then, by all means, request it. And when you do, make it clear your work will suffer if access is denied.

If you don't need the information, don't ask for it. Some managers feel an ego boost from being able to access classified material. If you need to know, then find out. If you don't, don't.

Once the decision is made to ask for restricted information, a leader should review the next questions.

2. *Is all the information required?* If you can get along with only partial disclosure, then do so. Do not delve further into classified

material than required for immediate needs. The more you limit access, the more protection you afford the information. Take only what you must have.

3. *Does the entire group need the data?* Can a few use the information without revealing it to the group? This is an extension of the need-to-know concept, but shows the logical sequence of security as applied to a group.

If everyone on the team needs access, again, do not hesitate. The information is either needed or not. If it is, your group can't move forward without it.

Match the degree of need with the level of classification. The higher the classification of secrecy, the greater the need to know in order to have access.

CLEARANCES

Many organizations have set policies dictating exactly who can and cannot be cleared for access to classified material. Other organizations do not.

If your firm has such a practice, follow the rules to the letter. Do not confuse your task of leading a group or participating in a meeting where classified material is shown with deciding that every member of the group should be cleared to see it. The problem of clearances, in terms of groups which meet on a regular basis, is that some members might not be cleared. Normally, limited exclusion won't occur, because admission to the group, if management knows classified material will be exposed, requires a clearance of a given level.

The problem of only partial group clearances usually arises when the need for access was not foreseen and develops out of one or more lines of discussion. Leaders should make all reasonable effort to persuade those granting clearances to include the entire group. If one or more attendees is not granted clearance, their worth in the decision-making process will be lost. Worse, their sense of belonging will be badly crimped. To be told your organization does not trust you sufficiently to see certain material does not engender loyalty.

Usually, a rejection of clearance is couched in other terms, such as a rule requiring two years of service with the organization before application, or other nonpersonally directed regulation. No matter what the reason, the effect is the same. The feeling of rejection is only made stronger by those not granted clearance seeing fellow managers so honored.

The clearance, for all potential harm it may cause, is still the second pillar of a security system. Leaders should not forget that imposition of the clearance system removes their responsibility for who sees what material.

If an organization has no clearance policy, then the team leader is usually responsible for deciding who sees the material, and the information is released to the leader, who then passes it along to the group. In this system, the leader has accepted responsibility for the classified data. If there is a leak, management generally holds the leader responsible. Be aware of the added responsibility.

Management's position on this "leader-responsible" approach is not out of place, in that it is the leader who must ask for the data, the leader who is responsible for dissemination of the material, and the leader who best knows the people in the group. Even so, more than one manager has been surprised when called to account for another's revelations of classified data.

DISSEMINATION OF CLASSIFIED MATERIALS

One more intelligence axiom: A manager who only knows part of a secret is not as dangerous as one who knows all of the secret.

As a leader, you must decide who gets what classified information. If at all possible, divide the material, so each manager receives what he or she needs for individual problems, but no one person, other than yourself, has access to all. If this isn't feasible, do what needs to be done. But study the situation to make doubly certain there is no way to parcel out the data and still attain first-class results.

Dissemination of data, regardless of organizational policy, requires the following:

1. *Acknowledgment of Receipt.* As leader, you probably had to sign for the material when you received it. Keep your records straight. Get a signed statement from every person who receives the material from you. This statement is a simple acknowledgment that the individual received the material at a given time on a certain day, and is aware of the level of classification.

Two reasons for signed statements: Your records will show your disposition of the material, and of equal value, the person receiving it from you will be reminded of the confidential nature of the information. There is nothing like signing your name to a receipt to get your attention.

2. *A Clear Understanding the Material Is Classified.* Unlikely as it seems, many leaks are traceable to carelessness at the time of transferring the material from one pair of hands into another.

At the time of transfer, make sure the person to whom you are passing the information understands the material is classified, knows the level of classification, and accepts accountability for the material. A statement to this effect, as noted earlier, should be included on the receipt form.

3. *Return of the Material.* When the need to use the information is over, the material must be returned to the leader. The leader acknowledges this by giving the manager a counter-receipt, stating acceptance of the material from that manager on a certain date at an indicated time.

Signing classified documents in and out may seem tedious, but experience proves this elemental process is effective in maintaining security.

COPYING CLASSIFIED DOCUMENTS

When classified material is in your hands, be leery of making copies. Many documents are stamped "Do Not Copy." Even in the absence of such a stamp, don't assume any classified material is copiable.

There may be a desire to make copies of a page of figures, for instance, so others in the group can more easily follow your discussion, but reproduction should be avoided for two reasons: First, you may not get every copy returned. And second, not everyone in the meeting might have need-to-know status meriting a complete copy of the classified page.

A better technique is to make an overhead projection cell from the material and show it on a screen. The overhead cell, along with the original from which it is produced, stays in your possession. The information is offered to the group, and no one retains the full array of numbers on the page. If necessary, the projection cell may be highlighted, or a mask can be placed over noncontributory areas.

NOTE IN PERSONNEL FILE

Many group leaders find it a good practice to have a note, indicating the individual is in possession of confidential material, placed in each manager's personnel file. If a manager leaves, those in charge of personnel matters will see the note and make appropriate checks to confirm recovery of the material before the manager is released.

Some leaders ask personnel to file the receipt of material that has been signed by the manager, in that manager's personnel file. In any case, some notation in the file, opened when classified information is passed to the manager and closed when it is retrieved, is a sound idea.

SECRECY AGREEMENTS

Organizations vary in the use of secrecy agreements. State laws vary, too. In general, though, it is not unreasonable for an organization to ask managers who have access to classified material to promise not to reveal that material to others while in the employ of the organization, or for a given number of years after termination of employment.

Many organizations apply the secrecy agreement to the entire proceedings of a group when that group works on classified projects or accesses confidential material.

Reactions to secrecy agreements vary, so if a large group is requested to sign one, there will probably be some dissenters. Here again, the effectiveness of a productive group can be curtailed.

RESTRICTIONS TO MINUTES AND AGENDAS

The meeting agenda may be restricted if classified material is to be discussed at your meeting. No reference to the classified nature of the discussion should be made on the agenda, and its distribution should be more carefully controlled during sessions in which sensitive material is under review.

Many effective managers add a code at the bottom of the agenda, to remind attendees that restricted matter will be disclosed during the meeting. This usually takes the form of initials, such as "C.M.U.D." (Classified Material Under Discussion) or "R" (for Restricted). A cryptic note seems a little dramatic, but is a good psychological stimulant for attendance. It's human to want to know something others do not.

In minutes, be direct. Note that there was a discussion of sensitive material and positions were taken. No reference to the nature of the material should be made—just the plain notation of the happening. And if a decision was made which in and of itself is classified, the record of that decision must be couched in terms that will protect the information. The minutes, as well as the agenda, are extensions of the meeting itself, yet they are not classified in most cases, and are seen by relatively large numbers of people, including support staff, secretarial associates, members of the reproduction center, and so on. It is the leader's responsibility to be sure neither minutes nor agenda reveal restricted information. (Another strong argument for the group leader having a direct connection with the preparation of minutes.)

CODE NAMES

Code names seem a bit romantic, but are a way of life even outside the area of information restriction. They can be fun, too. More than one group has named its classified projects after members of the group, referring to them as "Ralph's Project" or "Jennifer's Inquiry."

Use code names if they are needed. It's a quick, nonrevealing shorthand to reference a program and can appear in minutes, on the agenda, or in appropriate correspondence, including meeting memos. Don't let the feeling of sophomoric posturing deny you this useful method of referring to sensitive work.

EGO

Inner-organizational activities to keep certain information restricted in terms of access and distribution, can have positive effects on ego and manager morale, as well as the less attractive negative side-effects mentioned earlier in this chapter.

To be selected as one of a few to have access to certain sensitive materials is a boost to the ego. It is a statement from the organization's top management that you are worthy of special trust and your views on matters in which you have expertise are desired and respected. A leader should remember this and use it as a force to keep the group productive and cohesive.

This same positive attitude is perhaps the best single way, when coupled to a person's honesty, to control classified material. When trust is placed in an individual, the normal reaction is to try to be worthy of that trust. Trust begets responsibility. And only responsible managers will exercise proper care of secret materials.

As a group leader, do not be afraid to play on this egocentric feeling. It can be molded into a strong ally.

DISCUSSION RESTRICTIONS

If the entire group is cleared to review classified materials, there should be few or no restrictions on any discussion of that material. Leaders will find that some members of the group have been overly impressed by the implanting of a need not to disclose the sensitive matter and will not take part in the discussion. Watch for reluctance, and if necessary, meet with those individuals in private to resolve this problem. Do not discuss this with the group as a whole since there are also probably those who feel "all this secrecy stuff is a joke," or "it's disgraceful," so you may be opening the possibility of slack control of material in your care.

The leader's role in getting everyone in the group to a level of maximum participation can be difficult when classified material is first used by the group, but will grow easier as each manager becomes familiar with the procedures.

The leader's opening statement can focus on this problem, but a better technique is that of example. If the leader shows no hesitation in using the information in discussion, others will follow.

AFTER-MEETING FOLLOW-UPS

The leader should end each meeting in which classified materials have been discussed with a reminder of the confidential nature of that material.

After adjournment, there is, especially if the session was highly productive, a kind of post-meeting euphoria. During this period, attendees may be inclined to tell someone of their achievement and satisfaction with the accomplishment. In doing so, classified material may be inadvertently revealed. Counter this, not by having meetings which fail to give such satisfaction, but by encouraging everyone to remain after the session for a moment of relaxation. This provides the leader an opportunity to be certain that unresolved disagreements arising in the discussion do not become open topics of conversation in the corridors.

REALISTIC EXPECTATIONS

When more than one person knows a secret, there is no way to keep that secret. This is true even in wartime governmental actions to protect military information. Most security experts understand that classifying information is a way to retard its dissemination. By slowing the process, time is gained for exclusive use of the information. There are no absolute secrets, and the goal is to delay the flow of information—not completely prevent it.

In meetings, classified material presents problems for the leader as well as participants. These difficulties should not be magnified out of proportion to the true intent of the security system. Regrettably, in many instances, the impediment to information outflow also hampers decision making.

The question of secrecy is a serious one, in terms of impact on the group. It is not, however, an insurmountable difficulty. By using the information here, an effective leader can foresee pitfalls, understand the need and methods for protecting information, and be self-confident in its use.

It is imperative the leader is never placed in a "watchdog" position over meeting participants. Leaders are present to lead, not act as security police.

11 | Meeting Manners

$\mathbf{M}$anners are a code of proper conduct. Manners are maps of behavior for certain situations. Manners are necessary for a group to have reasonable, civil exchanges and remain cohesive during discord. Manners have strong historical roots and usually lag behind the current beliefs and thinking of the society they control and serve.

Recent sociological behavior alterations have given rise to new problems with manners used in business. This is, in itself, not surprising, because manners within a group are in a state of constant evolution, to better reflect the attitudes of that group.

Some forces that forge manners may shape them in ways that conflict with previous custom. When abrupt change occurs, individuals in the group are confused and unsure what to do in given circumstances.

WHAT SHAPES THE MANNERS OF A MEETING

Manners in a meeting reflect the ages of those present. If the individuals are about the same age, their manners will be more alike than if some attendees are in their 60s and others under 30.

It would be simple to state: "Good manners are good manners anywhere, under any conditions," but this is not true. Good manners are

115

those perceived by observers as being "good." Regional differences induce a large acceptable variation. Nonetheless, there are some standards. And there are certain courtesies that deal with one person's actions affecting another's state of being.

For meetings, there is some degree of manner stabilization. Or, at least, there are guidelines to help determine which set of manners to use.

One fundamental rule is: All present in a meeting are equals insofar as their making a contribution to that meeting. This is true regardless of sex, age, position, and so on. Once the meeting begins, all present are equal, in terms of right to express views, take positions, and vote on decisions. This position of equality must exist for a meeting to be effective, not the converse, where some attendees are considered more equal than others.

SMOKING

The image of smoke-filled meeting rooms where far-reaching decisions are made is common enough to have entered our folklore and language. In today's world, however, the picture presented by a smoke-filled room is passe. Smoking is on the decline, especially in business surroundings. Increasing numbers of upper echelon executives do not smoke. And if the truth were told, do not want their managers to smoke, either. So smoking in the business world, among upwardly mobile management, is waning.

As leader, you become the arbiter on smoking in your group. If all are smokers, there is no problem with smoking during your sessions, although there may be an increased risk of medical problems among the group. If no one smokes, there is again no problem. Smoking is not a concern.

If part of the group wishes to smoke and part not, then there is an obvious difficulty. The leader is responsible for solving this dilemma.

The leader's first act should be to reference local and federal laws pertaining to smoking. There is a growing body of regulations concerning when and where smokers may light up. Human resources or personnel will probably have the latest updates and be able to tell you how they affect your group.

Next comes organizational rules and customs. These will vary across the nation, but more and more are limiting smoking to specified areas, regardless of the usually lesser legal requirements.

These two sources may well serve to resolve any conflicts between the need of smokers and comfort of nonsmokers, and a simple announcement, stating there will be no smoking because of legal or organizational policies, will suffice.

If smoking is permitted in meeting rooms, the leader should designate a smoking and nonsmoking area for each meeting. The smoking zone should be well-ventilated, and drafts should not carry the smoke toward nonsmokers. No one will be satisfied with this "solution." Nonetheless, it's the only compromise that protects everyone's right. Recent studies indicate "passive" inhalation of smoke in the air can be as harmful as "active" smoking. Opponents and protagonists disagree, but more and more often, nonsmokers are sensitive to the issue of smoke in the air.

A leader wants everyone in a meeting to be comfortable, relaxed, and sufficiently at ease to bring out maximum participation. Smokers and nonsmokers seem less and less able to attain these states when confined in a room with each other.

Another answer, although smokers will not concur with this position, is to ask each attendee to refrain from smoking during the meeting. Smokers may feel a certain aversion to being asked not to smoke, but few smokers are unable to go an hour or so without smoking. If smoking is allowed, smokers should be encouraged to maintain clean, odor-free ashtrays.

It is surprising how much regional bias there is in the smoking controversy. If you attend meetings in other parts of the United States, you will be confronted with a noticeable variation in smoking custom. It is an equal problem for smokers and nonsmokers alike—and a real dilemma for group leaders.

REFRESHMENTS AND SERVICE

Another potential issue is found in the service of refreshments. Once again, regional variation is exhibited.

In the American tradition, and that of many other parts of the world, women have been seen as homemakers, which assigns them the role of food preparation and service. As more women enter the managerial level, meetings become increasingly mixed sexually, as opposed to the all-male preserves they once were.

This duality of roles has placed stress on the previously accepted stereotype of the woman as server of food. The simplest solution is do-it-yourself service. Or, except in situations such as a breakfast session or lunch meeting, have no food or snacks available.

In some organizations, secretaries serve refreshments prior to a meeting. Unless you, as leader, are sure of the attitudes of each individual present, do not encourage this practice, as you run the risk of developing an internecine war which will definitely impair the effectiveness of any group.

If refreshments are mandated, let everyone serve him or herself. And be sure the refreshments are in place before your first attendee arrives. Or have them brought in by individual participants, not the female secretarial staff. Alternatively, use the catering function of your firm or an outside, professional catering group.

UPPER MANAGEMENT PROTOCOL

The president of your organization is visiting your meeting. As leader or participant, you have a few customary obligations. Unless everyone present is known to the president, nametags or tabletop nameplates will make your chief officer more at home. Struggling for someone's name is not any way to feel comfortable.

It is the leader's job to be certain each attendee is introduced to a visiting dignitary. It is each participant's job to make certain he or she has been introduced, and after introductions, not dominate the visitor's time.

The leader should stick to the subject of the session and see to it members of his or her group do likewise. Some cannot resist the temptation of bringing up other, nonrelated, often personal problems, for arbitration.

If your dignitary is traveling with a guest, a secretary or assistant, be sure this person is included in all introductions and is seated at the table in accordance with the dignitary's wishes.

CHAIRS AND DOORS

Follow company policy in the area of men holding chairs for women attendees and men opening doors for women. This custom is under rapid change in business, moving away from the previous norm of male-female courtesy. Still, in many parts of the United States, men are expected to allow women to be seated first and always to open and hold doors. Even in meetings. If you are sent to meet in other geographic areas, observe and follow local custom. Awareness is necessary for male and female participants.

PROFANITY

Use of profanity in meetings is accepted in parts of our nation. In others, profanity is used freely if all present are male. In still others, profanity is not used and is not appreciated. As a leader, you must get the most from your participants. Certain managers, male and female, from selected areas of the United States, have grown to accept profanity in business meetings and, indeed, express themselves normally in this fashion.

No rule except local practice. And the leader should do that which makes the group effective.

AREA CLEANUP

It is the group's responsibility to leave the meeting area as it was found. So the group should act in unity to pick up after itself, even if there is a professional cleaning/housekeeping staff. The leader should encourage this practice.

MASCULINE REFERENCES

This does not refer directly to references about masculinity, but that is part of the problem. Traditionally, men and women have been thought to have different interests. These interests lead to the use of jargon in the normal expression of opinion or feelings.

Many businessmen tend to use sports-oriented terms. "We'll end-run 'em," or "Let's punt," or "That's a home run," are examples of sports-speak. Terms in actual use are more esoteric.

Women in business have learned the meaning of many of these phrases, and may even use them in expressing a position. But other women regard this practice as sexist and are offended. A leader cannot be responsible for jargon used by participants, but can guard his or her language, so as to set an example, and not create an irritant for any participant.

COMMON COURTESIES

A meeting room is not a battleground. It is not a place to attempt settlement of vendettas. It is a place to hold meetings. Productive meetings. And neither warfare nor revenge have a place in the meeting room.

Tempers may rise, expressions of position harden, and hostile looks can be exchanged in the heat of discussion. None of this is reason to forgo common courtesies, ignore protocol, or impose yourself, in any way, on a fellow participant.

Common courtesy, as recognized in your area of the United States, is not left outside a meeting room. You owe respect to others. They, likewise, owe it to you.

A leader should watch for lapses of common courtesy, however it is defined, and respond to those lapses in order to maintain civility.

An orderly meeting environment is productive. A discourteous meeting environment discourages productivity.

SEXIST VIEWS/RACISM

Many male managers have expressed resentment against the wave of women entering managerial ranks. Many female managers feel they are having to "make it in a man's world." Many managers don't feel either way, accepting male and female associates in terms of capability as opposed to sex.

Sexist attitudes can, and have, wrecked groups. At the least, sexist attitudes stifle expression, breed hostility, and kill the ability of an otherwise able group to make decisions.

The answer to sexist problems is not to confine membership of a group to all men or all women. The answer is to bar sexist views, held by males or females, from your meetings.

A leader should appraise his or her group for sign of this emotional bias and, if present, work with those holding such feelings. It is not a leader's task to psychoanalyze or counsel the emotional view-points of participants. It is a leader's job to create a proper environment for creative exchanges. This environment is damaged by emotional bias and expression of that prejudice during meetings.

The leader is responsible for stopping biased statements. If an attendee persists in this discriminatory behavior, after discussion with the leader, that person is harmful to the meeting's progress and should be removed.

This is true for racist attitudes, as well. Racism has no place in business meetings.

Each mind in attendance brings a fresh viewpoint. Each mind enhances the possibility of the group's success.

MEETING BALANCE

Important principles should be stated more than once, because by repetition, they become firmly implanted, so once more:

A leader must try to develop maximum participation from every attendee at every meeting. That, and creating an atmosphere conducive to such participation, and keeping discussions on track, are the main tasks of a leader.

If this means dealing with regional variations in customs, and standards, so be it. The leader's responsibility remains.

In some parts of the United States, women have been encouraged to hold back their opinions. Many female managers have difficulty in expressing themselves in a mixed-sex group of peers. Leaders must watch for this reluctance to speak, identify it, and help the manager overcome these feelings. In meetings, everyone is equal.

Across the United States, male and female managers have problems in taking a stand that differs from their superior's. Leaders have to watch and help reticent members overcome their constraint.

Shy managers are less likely to contribute. Outgoing managers are likely to overwhelm and dominate a discussion. The list of causes relating to meeting imbalance is long. Leaders must detect these influences and bring the meeting into balance. That's part of the job.

PERSONAL REMARKS

Personal remarks were touched on in Chapter 5. It is worthwhile to bring this up again, under manners. Avoid personal remarks.

If you are group leader, stop them as soon as they begin. Do not allow the practice of making personal remarks to become entrenched, as you will find it harder to stop, the longer the practice continues.

Include in personal remarks those comments of a personal nature made directly by one attendee to another, comments from one participant to another about an attendee, and any action, facial expression, or overt display which tends to belittle or deride.

No one performs well under fear of having his or her efforts ridiculed. Aware of this, some managers use scoffing as a means of attack or intimidation.

In business conversation, any manager may express doubt about another manager's facts, but no manager has the right to mock or personally insult other employees of the organization. If a leader is faced with this behavior, there is a four-step process which is effective in correcting the situation.

First, the leader should directly halt the errant behavior. The word "directly" is important. The leader should be open and blunt. For example:

> John, that reaction is uncalled for. I don't appreciate it, and I'm sure the rest here agree. We have a lot to do. Let's keep this professional.

A leader must voice his or her open displeasure with the attendee's behavior, because those derided need support at that instant if the situation is to be saved. Be friendly, not angry, but firm, and possibly a little disappointed.

Second, the leader should immediately apologize, on behalf of the group, to the person who has been ridiculed. Don't make a major production of the apology, but make it and make it clear you mean it. For example:

> Roger, I'm sorry. On behalf of the group, I'd like to apologize for John's reaction. It has no place in this meeting.

Third, get the participants back into their discussion as quickly as possible. Return to business by forcing the victim to pick up where the meeting was interrupted.

Roger, start again, at the plan for financing the improvements.

The leader names a point just prior to the spot where the interruption occurred, and guides the injured party back to the subject.

Fourth, when Roger begins, the leader should look John, the offender, directly in the eyes. Don't make this a dare, but be resolute.

At this point, the leader must try to judge the amount of harm which has been done and use every effort to keep the discussion moving.

At the end of the session, the leader might remind all present that the meeting concerns business and there is no room in successful business for personal remarks.

We're all in this together. What we do, we do for our common good.

When the meeting is over, forget the incident, except to note it in your evaluation process, so if it happens again, you'll recall the previous occurance and the person who precipitated the event.

INTIMIDATION

Unlike personal remarks and other tactics, intimidation is a widely used meeting technique. Sufficiently common, in fact, to be considered by many a valid ploy during a discussion.

There is a difference between going into a meeting knowing what you want to accomplish and going into a meeting to get your own way. Having a goal when the meeting begins and striving to attain that goal, while being a good participant, is different from exercising no scruples in protecting a position.

Intimidation is one of the most common, in more ways than one, methods of trying to force an opinion onto another person. It is essentially an emotional process, in which sufficient fear is generated in one participant by another to cause the nervous attendee to acquiesce to the intimidator's demands.

Intimidation does not work without fear. The usual method of generating the needed cowed response is to appear to be angry. Some merely return anger. Others, however, react fearfully, and the first step towards intimidation is taken.

The leader who watches for anger is also blocking the intimidation technique. And it should be stopped. Fearful individuals do not make good participants. And the individual who will deal with others on such an intense emotional level in a business meeting is not serving the group.

Another method to intimidate a participant comes from taking a superior position, then talking to the person to be intimidated as if he or she were inferior. If there is a sense of inferiority between intimidator and the intimidated, this will work.

In a meeting, everyone is equal. It's the leader's task to establish balance in the discussion and to maintain this sense of equality in order to ensure effective exchanges.

A third intimidation technique relies on ridicule. People react differently to ridicule as they do any stimulus. Many will be intimidated by the person delivering the derision. Banishing ridicule is another task of the leader. In fact, intimidation springs from the very acts a good leader must find intolerable.

So what happens in the real world? If the leader can be intimidated, attendees skilled in such tactics can control the group. If it becomes apparent the leader of your group is intimidated by another attendee, you have to decide to act against this, leave the group, or load your career with a record of service on an ineffectual committee.

Anyone who leads by intimidation is doomed to lead a group which will make poorer decisions than a properly led group. Think about that and you'll see why. The intimidator is forcing ideas onto everyone, then forcing acceptance of those ideas. The intimidator is the only idea source.

People who consistently use intimidation tactics to win discussions are not easily dissuaded from this practice. Intimidation seems to be a natural need in some and is learned by others. Do not rely on intimidators to change their style. It's best to cull rather than continue with the problem.

Intimidators, for all their apparent lust for control, do not normally make good leaders. In positions of leadership, they tend to use their authority, no matter how limited, as a base for more intimidation. If you have the misfortune to be assigned to a group led by an intimidator, do all you can to change assignments.

LEAVING THE MEETING EARLY

No matter how careful you are with your schedule, situations arise which cause time conflicts. A session, that has never lasted more than an hour and was only planned for 30 minutes, goes on for an hour and a half. Your afternoon, which you always leave free the day of your regular weekly meeting, is jammed. A new sales manager is in from the field. Joan, who broke her schedule to accommodate you in setting up another meeting, has asked you to attend a conference in her office at 4:00 P.M. And you still have 10 telephone calls to return.

There are times when you must leave a meeting in progress. When you have to go, then go. But before you leave, be sure you take a few special steps. If You are the Leader:

1. *Explanations and Rearrangements.* Understand that your leaving, if you just excuse yourself and depart, can end the productive portion of the meeting. Your people may also fall into disharmony or lassitude. The thought that you are so uninterested in the topic as to simply excuse yourself, can kindle all manner of long-term difficulties.

Obviously, you ought not leave without explanation. The trick is to make the explanation early, at the beginning of the meeting, in your opening statement. There are several directions. Each is sound. Your choice depends upon the amount of business, and the importance of that business, to be conducted.

A leader may say that due to unusual circumstances, he or she will be forced to leave at exactly 3:15 P.M. And it would be helpful if all vital issues could be reviewed by that hour.

If the preliminary pre-meeting activity is cut short, significant time can be gained. Which adds to time allotted for matters before the group. When the predetermined departure time arrives, end the discussion, adjourn, and leave.

If the business at hand does not allow for this, then ease the situation by rearranging the agenda in the opening remarks, after explaining your need to be absent, and deal with the most vital concerns first. Agenda shuffling may excite some of those present, but the main issues will be discussed in your presence.

If neither of the above is advisable, then during the opening remarks, ask another person to chair the entire meeting. Don't spring your request as a surprise. Prearrange this appointment. Do not change leadership when you leave. Let your appointee take charge from the beginning. You make the opening remarks, name the pro-tem leader, and turn it over to him or her. This provides for better continuity at your departure.

2. *Apologies.* Understand you have set a bad example, no matter how tight your schedule, by leaving a meeting which you insist others attend.

The best way to correct this impression is through a meeting memo that offers an apology. If possible, your having to leave should be associated with an upper echelon executive's demands or needs.

Another technique is to personally see each member of your group and tell them you are sorry. A short, properly worded apology can help future attendance.

> I believe our meeting is the most important part of my week. It bothers me when I have to do something else. You know the feeling.

If upper management is the cause, or partially the cause, say so in the meeting. Everyone understands that a superior's urgent request can take precedence.

3. *Responsibilities.* Understand that deadlines still have to be met. If your group was to have a report on an officer's desk at a given time, it still must be there. And your responsibility to have it there is greater, not less, because you were forced to leave the meeting.

When departing early, take deadlines in consideration and carefully plan how they will be met. If special instructions to the group are required, try to reduce them to a memorandum, which you can leave, and discuss them in your opening statement.

Finally, be certain everyone knows his or her responsibilities, so no confusion exists over what needs to be done by whom, by when. As a Participant:

1. *Resolution of Schedule Conflicts.* Understand your leaving will reduce the abilities of the group. Exhaust all other possibilities for resolving your schedule conflict before deciding to leave a session early. If there is no other solution, then that's business, and you must go.

2. *Prearrangement of Departure.* Talk with your group leader prior to the meeting and arrange to leave early. Your group leader will appreciate knowing you have to depart and can adjust the agenda to allow you to make any presentation or offer any thoughts prior to your leaving.

Check with the group leader before the session. A telephone call prior to the meeting assembly is better than waiting until the last minute to declare your intention of early departure.

3. *Arrangement for Coverage.* Have a participant cover for you by taking notes. It is helpful to explain your specific areas of interest in a discussion, so special attention can be paid by the note-taker even though his or her interest might lie in another direction.

Again, it's better to have your note-taking arrangements made before the meeting, rather than trying to set them up at the last minute.

Your conversation with the leader will be better received if he or she knows you have someone monitoring the portions of the program with which you are concerned.

4. *Audio recording.* A small tape recorder, placed on the table unobtrusively and out of the way, will provide a good record of the session. Inform your leader of your desire to record, so he or she may tell the other participants. It disturbs people to find, as a surprise, there has been a tape unit tracing their every word.

In general, the rule for early departure from a meeting is early notification, to the leader or the group, and early preparation for someone to support your departure by covering those aspects of the session which you will need for next meeting preparation.

EMERGENCY DEPARTURES

If an emergency occurs while the meeting is in progress, and your presence is imperative to help settle the crisis, then obviously, you have to leave the meeting without preplanning.

If you are the leader, quickly appoint someone as leader pro-tem, and go. When the emergency is resolved, do not return to the meeting, even if it is still in progress, if you were absent more than a few minutes. If you are gone for a half hour, your return will bring the already hampered meeting to a halt, to fill you in on the discussion. This is one more distraction.

If you are only away for a few minutes, when you return, be sure to let the members of your team know the general nature of the emergency. All will be curious and relieving their curiosity will help them settle down.

Apologies are not in order when leaving for an emergency situation. A simple "Excuse me," is adequate.

If your are a participant and are called away, try to get someone to cover for you. Tell the leader you must leave, then go as quickly, as quietly, and as unobtrusively as possible. Your goal is to minimize interruption and disruption of any discussion in progress.

As a leader, be on guard against participants who frequently leave sessions before the end. This can become a rather bad habit and is disruptive to the group. If you have someone who abuses this privilege, then it behooves you to speak with him or her in private. Be willing to accept excuses and be sympathetic with the plight. But also be unwavering in your stance. You need that individual in the meeting and to keep him or her there, offer to help schedule the participant's time. Sympathy for a complex situation and a firm reminder of obligation to the group works better than rebuke.

SUMMARY

Manners are important. Especially in business meetings. The concept of "good" or correct manners varies regionally, so be prepared for interesting changes in the norm when you meet away from your home area.

Maintain good meeting manners, because good meeting manners make for better meetings.

12 | Meeting Room Setup

Meetings are held in a variety of surroundings, ranging from paneled boardrooms to small offices where someone has to sit on a desk. Most meetings, though, the formal kind, take place in what are called conference areas, furnished with tables and chairs.

The right furniture groupings, depending upon the type of meeting you have been asked to conduct, can help establish the proper meeting environment.

Room arrangements are endless, but there are some guidelines that will help avoid room settings that combat free exchange.

ROOM TEMPERATURE

Many managers believe a cold meeting room keeps attendees awake. Experiments by psychologists and physiologists, however, show warmer body temperatures produce greater mental activity. Opt for improved brainpower, which means warmer room. Remember, though, that even a small number of people in a confined space for an hour produce a significant amount of body heat. So if you start with the room at 72 degrees F. it will quickly become hotter. A warm, well-ventilated space is the best option. Rely on the excitement of the meeting to keep attendees awake.

ISOLATION

The meeting area should give a feeling of isolation, even if that feeling is only illusion.

In offices with the usual dry-wall partitions, meeting rooms need doors, that should be closed when a meeting is to begin. It's good for late arrivals to have to open a door to enter the room. The action adds to their discomfort and makes them less likely to repeat their tardiness.

In the typical "open office" system, which uses special modular panels to create work stations, meeting space can be made to seem more private by having no access to windows. A zone of brighter lighting can also be used to divide it from the balance of the floor.

Many offices designed on the open plan utilize modular conference areas for regular meetings in which nothing of a sensitive nature will be considered, and traditional walled-off conference rooms for discussion of private concerns.

CLEAN AREA

The meeting area must be clean. Nothing is more depressing, in terms of pre-meeting gathering, than arriving to find a messy room with partially filled styrofoam cups vying for tablespace with overflowing ashtrays. Add to this diagrams still on the blackboard, rumpled papers tossed towards the wastebasket and you have an unwholesome scene.

Recall the rule about cleaning up after yourselves? It would be nice if everyone recalled that rule. So if you are the leader, go to the room a little early. If it's a mess, do what you can to improve it before your group arrives.

If upper level executives attend a meeting you are leading, be certain the room is neat and clean. It needn't be sparkling or fancy, but it must be businesslike, orderly, and policed for cups, ashtrays, napkins, discarded notes, and the like. Neat and clean. An upper-level executive's first impression of how you conduct a meeting, your rapport with your group, and of your group itself, will come from the condition of the room. Regardless of how others left it, your reputation is being evaluated.

LIVING ROOM SEATING

If the session is to be an informal exchange of ideas or brainstorming to develop new concepts, consider doing away with tables and moving to a more casual living room seating. This works for six to eight people, then, in order for everyone to hear everyone else, the group forms a large circle and tables are a better option.

TABLE POSITIONS

Round tables are better than square or oblong tables. King Arthur knew what he was doing. At a round table, the distance across to another participant is less and the feeling of group involvement is heightened. It is also easier for everyone to see and focus on the speaker.

Business tables are usually square or rectangular, however. Of the two, square is better. Even a large square is better than a shorter rectangle.

Rectangular tables place two rows of seats, one along each side of the table, facing each other. This is an adversarial positioning of people. Worse, in a group of 12, with 6 to a side, the first and last attendees on either end are at least 15 feet apart. And neither can see the other without leaning far forward and craning the neck. This position is not conducive to open response in a discussion.

If a single rectangular table must be used, then alternate seating on either side, so as opposed to facing each other, eye to eye, which is a wonderful hostility builder, each attendee is facing a space between two others across the tabletop.

Two rectangular tables can be placed side by side to produce a square, or almost square, which is the second best arrangement. Consider this setup if the group size allows such a configuration.

Another room arrangement with tables, which helps in terms of breaking up facing lines of participants, is the "T" formation. One rectangular table is placed crosswise and another is positioned at right angles to form a "T."

The group leader and other presenters sit along the crossbar of the "T," with attendees staggered along both sides of the downstroke. Note "staggered" again. Alternating seating prevents the eye-to-eye faceoff. Direction of attention is towards the "top" of the "T," where the leader begins the meeting and those with presentations stand to make their points.

Another square configuration can be made from rectangular tables by placing them short edge to long edge, forming a square with an open center. This accommodates large numbers of participants, keeps everyone visible and allows good interchange, considering the size of the group. The space in the middle is left vacant. Presenters work from their places at the table.

A variation is the open square, which is especially useful if there are audiovisual materials to be shown. Remove one side of the square, leaving a "U" shape. The presenter stands at the open end of the "U," with the screen, and participants have a fine line-of-sight to the projection area. Projectors may be placed in the "U" between tables, preferably above the tabletop, to keep stray light from participant's eyes.

A final arrangement, also well suited to AV presentations, is the "V," with rectangular tables aligned in two converging lines which form a "V." Presenters work at the open end and participants sit along the outside of each table.

POSITION AT THE TABLE

As an attendee, you can either stand out from or vanish into the group, depending upon where you elect to sit relative to the position of the leader.

If you want to stand out, plan your seat so you speak across the bare tabletop, as opposed to over someone's head, when talking to the leader or chief.

Want to blend in? Reverse that. Out of sight can be out of mind, and by placing others between your position and that of the chief or leader, you achieve anonymity.

To stand out when the table is in the square configuration, select a seat opposite the leader or high-ranking dignitary. You will remain in sight. Sit one person away, on either side of the leader or superior, and you will be far less noticeable.

At a rectangular table, sit on the side opposite the leader or superior and two or three seats further down the table from that person. This gives you a clear expanse across the table and high visibility.

Seated same side of the table, second chair down from the leader, you blend into the group.

Round tables follow the same rule. Sit opposite the leader or superior for attention, second chair away for anonymity. It is harder to blend into the group if a round table is used, but it can be done.

It is not advisable to sit beside the leader or superior. Enthusiastic conversation at close range will cause you to appear a little too intense. Distance softens this impression, gives more room for use of hands to emphasize points, and allows you to watch other members of the group while addressing the power.

Remember seating by place cards? If they are used, do not forget to check where you have been seated, then move your card, if necessary, to stand out or blend.

MEETING KIT

Not part of the actual room layout, but included in the pre-meeting room setup, is the leader's meeting kit. Your organization may be different from most in this respect, but because meeting rooms are not usually any particular manager's responsibility, they are ill supplied with chalk, erasers, marker pens, wiping cloths, pushpins to hold displays to walls or easels, etc.

A clever leader assembles a kit of these necessities and brings it to each session. Since the materials are used on company business, they can come from the office supply center of the organization. Or, if allowed, purchased and placed on the expense account.

CORRECT NUMBER OF CHAIRS

Have the right number of chairs at the table. It is okay to have one or two too many, but not one or two too few. Too few chairs causes concern and delay while more furniture is located, transported, and put into place in the meeting room. No one takes much notice of too many chairs. Everyone notices when there are too few. Over-chair the table.

The ideal condition is to have exactly the correct number of chairs for those attending. Many upper echelon executives notice this detail.

SPECIAL TOUCHES

It doesn't take much: a small vase of flowers, typeset name cards for the table, tablecloths if appropriate, water and drinking glasses near visitors, clean ashtrays if there is to be smoking. Each touch demonstrates that your group is above the norm. Observers will take extra interest in your output.

The meeting room is important. It is more than merely a place to hold a meeting or shelter participants. It is part of the meeting environment and may be used to improve meeting productivity.

13 | Use of Audiovisual Techniques

Audiovisual (AV) presentations speed learn-
ing, aid in retention, and simplify complex concepts so they can be
more easily grasped. There is one caveat to that statement: Proper AV
presentations accomplish those goals; poor AV presentations confuse,
bore, distract, and retard learning.

It is not enough to plug in a slide projector and throw images onto
a screen, snap on an overhead projection unit and cast shadows on the
wall, pop in a videotape, or turn on a film projector. Proper use of AV
equipment is essential if the AV presentation is to achieve its goals. And
proper AV usage begins with an insight into how learning takes place.

MULTI-SENSE STIMULATION

We, each of us, learn through experiencing the world through our
senses. By hearing, seeing, touching, smelling, and tasting, we perceive
and define our environment.

There is a direct correlation between how quickly we learn and
the number of senses we employ in a learning situation. If someone
talks to us in a lecture, we hear the words and learn at a one-sense rate.
Seeing a word as we hear it adds sight to sound, so we learn faster—at a
two-sense rate. And we retain the information longer. Add more senses,
and we learn still faster and retain even better.

That's one use for audiovisual presentations. Information can be presented in such a way as to implant it into a viewer-listener's mind.

SENSE FROM NONSENSE

Many concepts are simple. Yet such concepts may be difficult to understand, because a series of logical steps must be followed to reach the concept. It is easy for humans to miss a few of those steps. So we often end up with garbled comprehension. Or no comprehension at all.

Audiovisual presentations can guide a listener-viewer from the beginning of an idea to its logical conclusion, taking every step and omitting none. So AV presentations make learning easier by ordering a sequence of facts or concepts and offering those facts or concepts in the same order each time the program is used.

CENTER OF FOCUS

You wish to present a budget. One way is to type the budget onto a sheet of paper, reproduce a sufficient number of copies to supply each participant, then with all referring to their documents, you review the information with the group.

Here is where problems arise. Each person is allowed to absorb the numbers at his or her own rate. So when one asks a question, others must move ahead or backwards through the figures, to find the questioner's place.

If those same figures are projected onto a screen in front of the group, and a presenter moves the group through the data at a unified pace, understanding is enhanced, portions of the numbers are not passed over, and everyone has a clearer picture of the situation when the presentation is complete. This saves time and improves learning, because each participant in the meeting has the same center of focus during the presentation. Of equal importance, the presenter can begin to form a position, through selecting what to emphasize or de-emphasize during the presentation.

CORRECT AUDIOVISUAL TECHNIQUES

Properly used, audiovisual techniques help a group be more effective. An understanding of correct AV techniques and use of the right AV equipment for each kind of presentation is important to anyone who wishes to develop meeting skills. This understanding begins with the room used for an AV presentation.

ROOM SETUP FOR AV USE

It seems almost too elemental to note that one desired quality in setting up for an AV presentation is to place the image where everyone may see it, without straining or having to sit in unusual attitudes.

Several table configurations, discussed earlier, lend themselves to AV viewing. The best are the "V" and the "U," or three-sided square. Both these provide excellent lines of sight from participants to the viewing area. And both have open spaces between the tables for setting up AV equipment.

The first rule in organizing a room for AV use, then, is: Make certain *everyone* can see the projected material. And can view it without having to contort into a hard-to-hold position. Even turning the head 90 degrees can become tiring in a 30-minute presentation. And tiredness draws the mind away from presented material, which defeats the purpose of the presentation.

LIGHTING

After the room is physically arranged, there are several other considerations. Among these is the amount of light needed. This is a compromise between a clear projected image and a fully dark room. Do not completely darken a room during a presentation. In a very dark room, the light source for the projector, no matter which type is used, becomes blindingly bright and irritating. Irritating participants is not the purpose of the presentation. At best, the light, which flashes when a slide changes or an overhead cell is removed and replaced, is distracting.

Dark rooms also strain the eyes, by forcing them to focus on a bright screen, surrounded by blackness. The difference in light intensity produces conflicting stimuli and eyes reflexively react and re-react, trying to adjust. This can quickly cause fatigue and associated discomfort.

Darken the room enough so that the person furthest from the screen can see the projected image clearly. This might require a twilight level of light, but never dark.

A second consideration for room light levels concerns the person presenting the material. Shy types seem to like dim lighting, so they can be anonymous in the near-dark and not have to see those to whom they are speaking.

That's the exact opposite of what is desired. The presenter must be able to see the faces of the audience because that's the only way to gauge understanding.

A presenter's dark vision is reduced by constantly focusing his or her eyes onto the projected image, so in very dark rooms the presenter does not see as well as the assembly. And the presenter must watch audience reaction to improve the presentation. This means that ideal room light levels are a compromise between attaining the best, brightest, clearest projected image and the ability of the presenter to actually see facial expressions of the viewers.

The room must also be sufficiently bright so that those who wish to take notes are able to do so without turning the greatest part of their concentration from the presentation. This is about the same light level the presenter needs to make eye contact with the spectators.

The ideal setting is just dark enough. If an error is made, make it on the side of too much light. The projected image will be softer but the presentation will improve.

There is a tendency, especially when using slides and slide projectors, to make the room quite dark and allow the presenter to read the presentation from the screen. This is not a good idea. Very dark rooms are conducive to sleep, and it is not uncommon to find someone blinking back to wakefulness when room lights are restored. Dark rooms after lunch especially promote drowsiness.

Make the room just dark enough to support a good image. And light enough for the presenter to see and participants to take notes.

TEMPERATURE

Many kinds of projectors emit significant amounts of heat while in use. If there are several presentations scheduled, try to have the room temperature lowered to offset this extra heat source.

PROJECTION SURFACES

Images can be seen when projected onto any light-colored surface, so in an emergency, any such surface will be adequate. For a planned meeting, however, there are preferable alternatives.

A screen is the best projection surface. Modern screens have been developed to enhance or brighten a projected image. This makes for sharper images at higher room lighting levels. And screens, especially the folding, portable variety, are designed to angle the projection surface into or away from the lens of the projector, thus alleviating the tendency of the picture to have slanted sides, called "keystoning," brought about by improper projector-screen alignment. Handling distortion problems will be covered later, but an adjustable screen is one way of overcoming projection shortcomings.

If no screen is available, a plain, nontextured white surface is next best. Large sheets of white paper can be quickly taped to a wall to form an impromptu projection screen. Seam lines between sheets can be overlapped at each joint a half-inch so they won't show enough to disturb viewers.

A textured white wall is third best. Texturing, such as spackling on wallboard, doesn't harm the image. It does, however, absorb light, so a darker room is required to maintain image quality.

It is a good idea to have a screen present in the room each time a meeting is held. Those making presentations will appreciate the thoughtfulness. And will do a better job with the presentation.

CORRECT AV EQUIPMENT

Selection of correct AV equipment is as important as having a correct room setting to present the desired information or concepts. Some AV techniques are better suited, say, to showing bright, colored graphs, than others. Some lend more informality than others. Some offer lower cost preparation of the visual materials to be projected.

AV equipment can be divided into categories. These include the slide projector (both silent and those coupled to an audiotape player, to provide syncronous sound); the overhead projector, which uses transparent cells as its source material; the strip film projector, which is a variation of slide projection and is almost always keyed to an audio source; motion picture projectors, which project silent and sound movies; and videotape units, which reproduce image and sound on a television screen.

All of these, because they are simple to use, are abused daily by managers who lack training in the proper way to get maximum effect from the equipment. Or who have selected the wrong category of equipment for the task.

Mastering meeting skills means mastering the correct use of AV equipment. Here is a comprehensive review of each of the major AV techniques. As you will see, this is not a difficult subject.

SLIDE PROJECTION

Most slide projection is done by passing a bright source of light through a specially developed 35-millimeter film frame. The film frame, produced by a photographic process, is encased in a metal, plastic, or pasteboard holder, so it may be handled, and so the projector can automatically move and retract one film frame after another, for ease of showing. The film frame and its holder are called "slides," and the projector that shows them is therefore a "slide projector."

Slide projectors come in various mechanical forms. The standard projector uses an open-topped circular tray to contain the slides in the order they are to be shown. When electronically activated, by a button on the side of the projector, a remote control connected to the projector by a cable, or a wireless remote controller, the tray rotates about a quarter of an inch and drops one slide into the projection position as the slide previously in that position is lifted back into the circular tray.

This sounds complex, but is more difficult to describe than to operate. In fact, once the slides are in the circular tray in the order in which they are to be shown, projecting them onto the screen requires the push of a single button. The hardest thing to remember about a slide projector is which button is used to move the tray forward, showing the next slide, or backwards, showing the slide just viewed. And the buttons even feel different, so you can tell them apart in the dark.

BENEFITS OF SLIDE PROJECTORS

Slide projectors produce images with great color and sharpness. The color is as intense as a photograph because it is a photographic image, so the hues are bright and vibrant. Black areas are truly black. Image sharpness, if the slide was properly produced, surpasses all other AV techniques except strip film, which is a variation of the slide presentation. Projected onto a screen, image sharpness is sufficient to allow the enlargement of typed numbers so that 50 or even a 100 seated managers can read them.

Slide projectors are programmable. The order in which slides are loaded into a tray determines the order in which they will be projected. Plan your talk, insert your slides in proper sequence, as determined by the order in which you cover points, and do your show. It's that simple.

Slides handle text as well as illustrations. This is a boon to the imagination. Show two slides of statistical information on family activities, then project a slide depicting a family enjoying those activities. Text and illustration can be a good way to make an important point.

Slides can simulate movement, by using stop motion sequence. Hands, for example, assembling a small part, can be photographed during various stages of the activity, then projected one at a time, in sequence, at any pace, to give a feeling of the assembly movements. An image can be made to grow or shrink in size, as one slide after another, presenting the same object larger or smaller, is flashed onto the screen. Slide motion can be dramatic.

Huge slide images are possible because the projected images of several slides can be overlapped to form one gigantic picture. The number of visual effects, including fade-in and fade-out of images and combinations of many images, is vast and impressive.

A prerecorded audiotape may be added to a slide projected image and can even be used to change slides, so the audience is presented with integrated sound and visual displays.

Because of their compact size and relatively light weight, slide projectors are portable and can be transported with the slide tray in position or stored in a separate container. The machines themselves are rugged and most models will withstand inadvertent abuse without malfunctioning or falling into misalignment.

Because of the slide projector's universal acceptance, many presenters only carry a tray of slides from one place to another, and use a projector available in the distant location. A slide projector is easy to set up, quick to repack, and is inexpensive.

All told, this has become the most popular method of projecting images onto a screen in meetings.

DRAWBACKS OF SLIDE PROJECTORS

Slide projection does not allow for actual movement, such as is available on videotape or motion picture film. Slide images are static. This can be dramatic, but for some uses, is limited.

A slide is produced from a single, 35-millimeter film frame by standard photographic processes. This means that compared to overhead projectors, each slide is relatively expensive and takes time to produce. New computerized equipment has cut both cost and time, but still the process is expensive when compared to overhead projection, which will be covered next.

Presentations using slides must be preplanned, at least to the extent of ordering thoughts and slides, so images coincide with the points you wish to make. This means slides are not particularly suitable for spontaneous presentations. Planning is required. So slides are generally used for more formal presentations.

PLANNING YOUR SLIDE PRESENTATION

Great slide presentations are visual experiences backed by audio to enhance the drama and make important points. Most slide presentations are audio presentations, in which the spoken word is backed or reinforced by a visual display. There is a big difference between those two approaches.

For business meetings, most managers work out the text of their remarks, then compose slides to fit those remarks by illustrating main points or clarifying concepts. This puts the person doing the presentation into the foreground, and the slides projected onto the screen in the background. There is nothing wrong with this approach, except the final product isn't imaginative and tends to become dull after a few minutes.

If this is the use to which you wish to put slides, the overhead projector is probably a better choice. Especially if the material on the slides consists of numbers, graphs, tables, or words.

Good slide presentations are more visual than verbal. Or, at the least, the audio portion of the presentation is enhanced by the visuals projected onto the screen.

CHECKLIST FOR CHOOSING SLIDE PROJECTION AS A PRESENTATION TOOL

1. *Meeting Size.* Slides are especially suitable for large meetings.

2. *Subject Importance or Program Repetition.* This presentation is extremely important or will be done on five or six separate occasions.

3. *Cost.* This presentation merits spending several hundred dollars for visual images.

4. *Necessity for Color and Sharpness.* This presentation cannot be done on an overhead projector because image sharpness

and vivid color are vital. (Full-color magazine ads are to be shown, for example.)

5. *No Need for Motion.* Actual motion is not required for this presentation.

The above criteria should dictate the use of slide projection.

DEVELOPING THE PRESENTATION

Books have been written on this single topic. For business meetings, unless there is a special reason, the rule is:

If you can't be exceptionally clever, be really simple.

Managers have tried a number of "cute" additions to their slide presentations, only to find that what seemed like a good idea while planning the presentation wasn't half so entertaining when the president or the chairman of the board was in the audience. Tricks, such as suddenly throwing the image of a scantily-clad body onto the screen as a break from a flow of numbers, seldom are well accepted and are always based on borrowed interest for shock value or humor. Do not borrow interest. Stick to the points you want to present and emphasize.

"Simple" doesn't have to mean dull. A simple presentation can be interesting because of the subject matter and the visual fashion in which it is offered.

If there are comparisons, use graphs and charts to visually support what you are saying. Use color to highlight certain figures with special significance and pop them out of a morass of numbers. Show photographs, even clippings from magazines, to visibly indicate the kind of people you are talking about. If your discussion centers on acquiring a parcel of land, show the land in question.

In short, use a visual to enhance, not just support, the audio portion of the presentation.

STEP-BY-STEP PROCESS

The following outline can be used in constructing a slide presentation. It is based on two concepts: First, if you cannot be extremely clever, be really simple. And second, the most exciting presentation is a visual display supported by the audio effects.

1. *Define Main Concepts.* Define the main concepts you wish to communicate.

2. *Define Conclusion.* Define the conclusion you wish viewers of the presentation to reach. If there is no specific conclusion, that is, the presentation is merely to present information, then define that fact.

3. *Order Logically.* Order the main concepts so that they logically lead to the conclusion you wish reached, or if there is no conclusion, order them in such a way that each concept stands alone or supports another.

4. *List Concepts.* Write or type each concept, and the conclusion, if there is one, onto 3"x5" file cards or a full size sheet of 8½"x11" paper. Each concept and conclusion should be isolated on a separate card or sheet. One card, one concept.

5. *Display the Program.* Place the cards or sheets horizontally on a table or pin them separately to a wall. You need space to place other sheets or cards above or below concept and conclusion sheets.

6. *Order Facts.* Start with the first concept you wish to present. List the facts which reveal that concept or lead to that concept, in the order you wish to present them. Example: The concept might be: "Operating Profits will be Adequate to Cover a $1,000,000 Expenditure Without Resorting to Outside Financing."
   Facts supporting that concept are:
   ∎ President's annual forecast.
   ∎ Actual performance, first three quarters.
   ∎ Operating profit as of beginning of fourth quarter.
   ∎ Fourth quarter historical performance.
   ∎ Large, already-filled order which will increase both fourth quarter income and profit.

7. *Categorize Facts.* Review the facts to see if any might be grouped into a single visual presentation. For example: (A.) The president's annual forecast and (B.) the first three quarters can be displayed together, using two graphs on the same slide. The president's forecast can also be shown with (D.) fourth quarter historical performance. Items (C.) operating profit and (E.) filled order, each stand alone.

8. *Draw Visual.* Imagine a way to show the relationships you wish the group to note and retain. Example: An X-Y axis line graph shows the president's forecast in red, the actual first three quarters' performance in black, and a series of yellow dots indicates historical fourth quarter levels. Draw the graph, in rough, on the upper third of a page.

9. *List Supporting Facts for Visual.* Below your graph, note in outline form what you will say when the graph is on the screen.

10. *Repeat for All Facts.* Do this for each fact you wish to show in support of the concept. If there is a fact which cannot be illustrated, use type to write the fact. Example:

Operating Profit: Beginning of Fourth Quarter:

$980,000 after estimated tax (point C. above)

    or

$290,000 order filled and delivered in third quarter. Costs have been taken in third* quarter. Income will be in fourth quarter (Point E above).

*Note: Use numerals for numbers you wish to enhance. Spell out all numbers for supporting information. In the example above, $290,000 is in numerals, "third" as in third quarter is in letters.

11. *Arrange Cards for Logical Conclusion.* Order the visual cards with the written summation of what you will say, in the same order as the list of facts you made (in step #6). Review what you will show and say. Does this clearly lead the audience to the concept you intend to communicate? For Example:

▪▪ Slide 1 shows the president's forecast has been conservative; the fourth quarter forecast, based on actual performance in the first three quarters, is projected to be in line with historical performance.

▪▪ Slide 2 shows operating profit at the beginning of the third quarter is almost a million dollars.

▪▪ Slide 3 shows there is over a quarter million more which will enter the company as income.

▪▪ Slide 4, which is the Concept Slide, reading: "Operating Profits will be Adequate to Cover a $1,000,000 Expenditure Without Resorting to Outside Financing," is logical and completes the presentation of this point. Repeat the process for each of the other concepts. (State the concept, align facts to support that concept, design a visual presentation of those facts, even if the presentation is only red type on a blue background, or white type on a black background, etc.), and add a summary of what you will say to the bottom of each visual sheet, remembering that each visual will be a finished slide.

When every concept has been covered, your presentation is reduced to a series of single sheets of paper. Each page represents a slide and your "script."

12. *Summarize.* If you wish to state a conclusion, prepare a final page. It is your last slide. If there is no conclusion, then prepare a single slide that reviews the information you presented. For example: Operating profits adequate to cover $1,000,000 cost of plant modernization are estimated at $500,000. Credit is available, if desired. (This is a summary of presented facts and concept.)

13. *Review Logic.* Review the presentation from first to last, to verify that each concept, and its conclusion is logically derived from the now-illustrated fact sheets.

14. *Review Visuals.* Review the presentation again, from first to last, to make sure you have illustrated each fact and concept clearly and that you cannot think of a more graphic way of showing the facts. When you are satisfied, go to the next step.

15. *Arrange Visuals from Opening to End.* Design a title slide. This is the first slide which will be projected onto the screen when you turn on your machine. This is probably the slide which will be viewed during your opening remarks.

Note: All effective slide presentations begin with a slide on the screen. This allows the audience to accustom itself to lower light levels, settle into chairs, focus on the screen, attune hearing to the audio volume, and get set for the presentation. It is a period of physiological and psychological adjustment. About 30 seconds should be allowed for the opening.

If your presentation calls for transferring audience attention from the screen to another portion of the room, to show, for instance, a three-dimensional model, a "black slide," which is an opaque piece of film in a slide mount or a cardboard "dummy" slide, is used to blank out the screen while room lights are intensified so the model may be discussed. When the model showing is over, lights are dimmed, and the next slide is selected.

If your presentation needs a black slide, indicate this on a sheet, write in the activity to be conducted while the black slide is "up," and put it in place with the rest of your sheets. Your goal is to have the complete slide presentation, from first slide to last, in front of you.

16. *Determine Length of Time for Each Slide.* Review the text for each slide, to determine how long the slide will be on the screen. There is no set rule for length of time a slide should be projected, because of variances in the interaction between the presenter and the screen image. For example: a slide is shown for three minutes. During that time, the presenter indicates several informative areas on the slide, illustrating a point. He or she refers to the slide 8 or 10 times. To the audience, this has the same value as 8 or 10 slides. Three minutes is not too long a period to show one slide, because of the interaction.

Note: If you intend to have a slide in the projector more than a minute, it is a good idea to glass mount the film in the slide holder. A glass mounted slide sandwiches the frame of film between two thin sheets of glass. (Normally a slide is made by merely slipping the film frame into a holder.) Glass gives the film added protection against intense heat produced by the projector's light source. Slides which are not glass mounted tend to buckle under such heat-affecting focus. Some may even melt if projected long enough.)

Example: A slide is shown for 20 seconds. It contains a great many numbers and some have been highlighted in red. The presenter says, "Please note the red numbers." Again, there is interaction between the audience, presenter, and slide. Twenty seconds is a short period of time.

Example: A slide is shown for 20 seconds. It has one four-digit number and no other copy. The same digit is mentioned one time by the presenter. Twenty seconds is too long with this slide.

Mentally place yourself in the audience at the meeting and try to see the presentation as you say it aloud. If the visual portion is too dull, brighten it up. Do not borrow interest by adding superfluous, nonrelated images. Do try to break a fact down into two or more parts, especially if that's the way you're going to talk the participants through it during the meeting. If a fact breaks down into three components, consider three slides. Three won't be necessary if you are interactive with the screen, but will relieve boredom if you are not.

17. *Prepare Script.* When you are satisfied with the visual display and it matches the text of your presentation, prepare a written script. You may or may not want to read your presentation verbatim. That's up to you. If you do wish to read it, then write out every word. If you do not wish to read it, only write the highlights you must cover. Example:

SCRIPT: FINANCE COMMITTEE
MEETING OF 16 OCTOBER '91

TEXT	SLIDE
THIS PRESENTATION DEALS WITH THE OPPORTUNITY TO CONDUCT EXPANDED PLANT DEVELOPMENT WITHOUT INCURRING ADDITIONAL DEBT.	#1—TITLE OF TALK "GROWTH WITHOUT DEBT"
A QUICK LOOK AT THIS YEAR'S PERFORMANCE.	#2—XY GRAPH PRESIDENT'S FORECAST— ACTUAL THREE QUARTERS— HISTORICAL PERFORANCE.

Note: The script is written in upper case only. Bigger letters mean easier reading in dim light. Or better quick referral, if the text is not for reading.

The Text portion covers what is actually said, or the gist of what is to be said, opposite a short description of the slide being projected.

When the topic changes, the visual will change. Alternatively the visual will be referred to and become interactive.

The completed script serves several purposes: First, it orders your talk. You can mentally experience the presentation you are about to deliver, and make changes as required.

Second, it allows you to get an estimate of the time required to deliver the presentation. And shorten the presentation, if necessary.

Note: Notice the operative word is "shorten." Never lengthen. If you can say it in less time, do so. Presentations do not need "fill." Neither do those to whom you are presenting. Asides and superfluous information only serve to distract from the points you wish to make.

Third, the script will, along with your rough slide drawings, serve as a guide for those who will actually make the slides. Knowing the context of the talk allows the slide makers to follow the flow, see what you want to present, and do a better job graphically.

Fourth, the script will allow someone else to load the slides in the order you want for your talk. Naturally, you will check slide order, using the script, before beginning your presentation, because it's your program and your responsibility.

Fifth, if approval is required, or confidential information is to be used, you may now submit the script for any required approvals.

18. *Discuss Script with Slide Maker.* Once the script is approved and/or you are satisfied with it, a copy, along with your rough renderings of what each slide will present, go to the slide maker. A meeting with this person is helpful in preventing mistakes.

Some organizations have internal operations for making slides. Others utilize outside sources. Both are fine and both can do a good job, if they know what you want. Neither reads minds.

Use the script, your roughs, and don't be afraid to speak up if someone suggests a color you do not feel is suitable. Explain your needs to the slide maker. Listen to suggestions, then decide. You must be the final arbiter because you are doing the presentation.

19. *Prepare an Audio Cassette (if Needed).* If your script calls for any sound effects or other audio aside from your voice, gather the material and have it put onto a cassette.

Note: In general, it is better, unless the slide presentation is elaborate, not to use an audio source other than your voice. If the material can be enhanced, however, recorded messages can be most effective.

Examples: Slide shows a housewife, while an audio tape, actually made during a research interview with a woman, answers the interviewer's questions.

Slide shows kids in a day-care center in a learning environment; audiotape made on the scene, has children reciting the alphabet.

20. *Check Slides for Mistakes.* Upon delivery of your slides, insert them in order into a slide tray and, without reference to the script, show them one at a time, about the same size as will be used in the presentation. Examine for spelling, punctuation, and so on. If there are any incorrect, and you still have time, get them remade. If not, use the technique described next.

After viewing the slides, have someone else, your assistant, a secretary, or an associate, view them with you as you read your script. The goal is to discover errors which, because you are so closely involved in the material, you will not be able to recognize. New eyes see old flaws.

Again, correct the improper slides, if there is time. If there is no time for correction, note the improper slides and specific errors on your script, and when the slide is projected, point out that here the word "transit" is misspelled. One or two mistakes in a 10 to 20 slide presentation won't cause you too much grief. It is better if all are accurate, but the cost of redoing mistakes, and the time element, may preclude this.

These 20 steps take you from the need for a presentation through the final tray filling prior to your appearance in the meeting. Experienced audiovisual users can cut steps out of the process. But it is not advisable. What time may be saved is at the risk of making a mistake or not presenting your material as clearly, concisely, and as interestingly as possible.

Numbering, Ordering, and Storing

When you sort your slides in the order in which they are to go in the projector, write a number in the corner of each one, indicating where it fits in the sequence. First slide is 1, second, 2, and so on.

Remember, because of the lens, if the slide in the projector is right-side up, the screen image will be upside down. Load your slides, upside down and backwards, in proper order, into the slide holder. Project each one, to make sure it is right side up and words read properly (not backwards). As each slide is approved, remove it, number the upper right corner, and replace it in sequence. After each slide has been numbered, project all again, to ensure the order didn't change, and for one final check to be certain the image is right-side up. Numbers on the slides will make reinsertion easier and faster, which is important if the slide holder is damaged or accidentally dumped.

When all your slides are in the cassette, lock them into place. The round tray type projector uses a large screw-down locking ring, which holds the slides ready and in position, and makes the tray an excellent storage container. Some managers go so far as to glue the lock ring into place, to prevent all chance of slides falling out.

SLIDE PRESERVATION

Keep every slide. Place them in one of the loose-leaf binders made for the purpose. You never know when you'll want a particular slide and discover you already have it in your collection.

LENSES AND PROJECTION

Modern slide projectors come with a variety of lenses, autofocus capabilities, and brightness levels to control the intensity of projection lighting.

The various lenses determine the size of the picture at different throw distances from the screen. The "throw distance" is the space between the projector lens and the screen or projection surface.

The goal is to fill the screen from the distance available between screen and projector. In practice, an image large enough to be seen by those in the room is adequate. If the lens you have will do this, then nothing more is needed.

Autofocus is necessary unless the presenter has a remote controller or is standing beside the projector. Which is probably the poorest position for the presenter to take, because he or she will be talking to the backs of innumerable heads. Backs of heads are not nearly as expressive as faces, so presenters should face the crowd.

With autofocus, the image on the screen is automatically focused by the projector. A remote, manual focus is also available, and in some ways preferable when showing detail-oriented slides. The problem with manual remote-control focusing is that standing close to the screen, the presenter has difficulty seeing the image as in or out of focus. With autofocus, the machine makes the decision and frees the presenter to present, not fiddle with equipment.

Adjustable light intensity is nice, but in a normal meeting room, usually unnecessary.

In most slide presentations, the projected image will not be composed of four parallel sides. The right and left edges of the slide will taper towards the top or bottom of the screen, unless the plane of the screen and the plane of the lens are exactly parallel. Many folding screens have an adjustment allowing the deployed screen to be tilted forwards or backwards to alleviate image taper, which is called "keystoning" because the image resembles the keystone of an architectural arch.

Do not concern yourself with this visual problem unless it is sufficiently pronounced to distort the material you project. Generally, in meetings, screens are placed three to five feet above the floor, so everyone can see the projected image. The slide projector is usually on a table, making the center of the lens closer to the floor than the center of the screen. Tilting the projector upwards, so the image strikes the screen, moves the lens out of parallel with the screen and causes the keystone effect.

HOT LIGHT SOURCE

Special bulbs used in slide projectors are very, very, very, very hot. The metal components surrounding the bulb for protection are likewise more than warm. How warm? Even after the lamp has been turned off for a while, it will sizzle skin. *Do not touch the bulb or its enclosure.*

WHEN YOUR PROJECTOR FAILS

If your projector fails, have another projector in reserve, switch the slide tray, and continue.

Do not believe that is it possible to change the bulb, without waiting 10 to 15 minutes. Have a spare projector. Don't bother bringing a spare bulb to a meeting. It won't be used.

Prolonging Projector Life

The bulb life in a projector can be prolonged by one simple act. When projection is finished, turn off the lamp, but leave the projector's cooling fan running several minutes. The cooling process extends bulb brightness, too.

In Summary

The slide projector is an exceptional piece of audiovisual equipment. It is rugged, reliable, and gives great images. The drawback is preparing the slides.

OVERHEAD PROJECTORS

These units take their name from the location of the projection lens, which is above (or overhead) the material being projected, as opposed to in front of that material.

Overhead projectors use acetate cells, which, for ease in handling, may be encased in cardboard frames. These cells are various sizes, but most are 8½ by 11 inches, the same size as a standard sheet of typing paper.

The image may be produced by photographic process, by using an office copy machine, or by hand, drawing directly on clear acetate. The image is not as sharp as a slide projector's, not as bright, and does not have the same intensity of color as that produced by slides.

The throw distance, from projection equipment to screen, is relatively short compared to slides, and the tendency to keystone the image is greater because the unit it bulkier and is therefore usually placed lower to clear sight lines.

With all these disadvantages, why are overhead projectors so popular? Because preparing material for projection is so simple: Type a sheet of figures. Run it through a copier, with a special, low-cost clear acetate sheet in place of paper in the paper tray, and you have a ready-to-use cell. Want to highlight? Mark directly on the cell with one of the felt-tip dye markers made for this purpose.

Does it look great? It's good enough so that many major presentations are made in this fashion. And it communicates as well as its clearer, more expensive cousin, the slide.

Another use of the overhead is creating images on the spot. For example, someone asks a question in a large assembly. The presenter uses a felt pen to write the question on an acetate sheet and projects it so all can see. And it remains projected, in front of everyone as a reminder of the question, while the presenter responds.

Writing the question onto the acetate gives the presenter time to frame an answer. Having the question visible keeps everyone's mind on the matter at hand.

The overhead projector is ideal for groups of 5 to 50, and in some instances, where lighting can be accurately controlled, even larger numbers, up to a hundred, can see the image.

BUILDING AN OVERHEAD PROJECTOR PRESENTATION

It's easy to build a presentation using the overhead unit. Follow the steps outlined for a slide presentation, until you come to the part about going to the slide maker. You can handle that task. Or your secretary can do it.

Draw your own graphs directly onto the clear acetate sheet. Using all caps or one of the special extra-large, bold-typefaces made for scripts, type the needed copy onto a white sheet, in the exact position you want it on the finished cell. (This is easy. Put the transparent cell over a sheet of white paper, use light pencil marks on the paper to show where copy should go, then type it there. Put the cell with the hand-drawn graph into the paper tray of a copier, copy the typewritten sheet, and *voilà,* text is in place.

Literally anything that can be copied by the machine can be turned into a transparency, which is another name for a cell.

Cells for overhead projection do not have to be mounted. You may place the acetate sheet directly onto the light stage of the overhead projector. In fact, many projectors provide a sharper image from unmounted transparencies.

For some reason, many users of overhead projectors put a sheet of plain paper between each cell. It appears this was originally done as a method of checking cell correctness. Line the transparency up with the original copy from which it was made, and any problems are immediately evident. Checking individual cells twice, as indicated in Step 20 of building a slide presentation will catch virtually all mistakes.

An error on an overhead cell isn't time consuming to repair. Just white-out the original page, retype, and make a new cell. Graphs may be copied from books or other papers, and recolored on the transparency by using felt-tip pens. Original graph lines come out black on the cell no matter what color is used in the original source material, so hand-added ink or dye serves as a colorful highlight.

The flexibility of the overhead also allows projection of some professionally made transparencies, which are shot in full color and photographically reproduced. A few of these will enhance a presentation, but overall, the images are less intense, with less vibrant colors than obtained with a slide projector. If you have material where color intensity and sharpness are crucial, the slide machine is a better projector.

Slide and overhead projectors may be combined in a single presentation, of course, and each assigned the task of doing what it does best. This makes for an interesting viewing experience.

Just remember there is no "dark slide" which works well with the overhead. The light source is simply turned off then on again when desired. Operating temperatures are lower than used for slide projection, so turning the machine on and off causes no significant problems. Also, because of the lessened temperatures, a cell may stay in place on the projection surface as long as you like, without damage.

COMMON FAULTS

There are two common faults found among even experienced uses of overhead projectors. The first deals with handling the cells or transparencies. Imagine this sequence. A cell is on the projection surface and is displayed on the screen. The presenter removes the cell. The screen goes bright white (or bright whatever color the screen is) as light from the projector, now projecting nothing, continues to beam. Then the screen shows a new image as the presenter places the next transparency onto the projection surface.

This is a natural method of changing cells, but is not a good presentation technique because intermittent flashing of the bright, imageless screen is distracting. Worse, it causes anticipation for what will appear next, which breaks the mind away from the presented material.

The proper method for changing cells is as follows:

Grip the cell on the projection surface between thumb and forefinger of one hand, and start to lift it away. At the same time, bring a new cell into place on top of the old one, and as the old one slides off the projection surface, the new one slips into place. This gives a continuous display on the screen without interrupting, attention-damaging white light, and provides a smooth transition from one cell to the next.

Practice putting one transparency in place while lifting the other away. After a few tries, you'll get the knack. It makes a recognizable difference in flow and smoothness of your presentation.

This one-on-at-the-same-time-one-comes-off technique also prevents the broken speech pattern caused by the other way of changing cells. As the speaker halts in mid-sentence while making the change, the audience is subjected to bright white screen and silence. Either one is not professional and together are distracting.

The second common fault is the constant fiddling some users of overhead projectors do to get split-millimeter precision in the alignment of the cells. This is unnecessary. As long as the copy in the projected image is reasonably horizontal with the top of the screen, it's fine. Your audience cannot be expected to twist necks in order to read a line of text that runs diagonally, but even rough alignment is sufficient to prevent that.

Take the old cell away, slip the new cell into place at the same time, glance at the screen to be sure it is relatively straight, and continue talking through the process without pause or interruption.

Stopping to slip the transparency an eighth of an inch lower on the right corner, a process which requires concentration and halts speech while the presenter studies the screen for exact placement, is far more interruptive to the flow of the presentation than having the line of type run slightly uphill.

If proper cell alignment is vital to your presentation, tape a strip of pasteboard to the lower edge of the projection surface, then use it as a "stop" for an edge of the cell, assuring alignment.

RIGHT SIDE UP

Unlike a slide projector, overhead units show what is on the projection surface without turning it upside down and backwards. Standing next to the projector, with a cell in place and the screen behind the presenter, the transparency should be readable. That is, right-side up, with type reading right to left. If this is true, the projected image will be correct. Many transparency sheets come with a narrow white band on one edge or with one cut corner, to serve as a guide. As a double-check, however, if you can read the cell and place it onto the projection surface so it is readable, it will show correctly.

NUMBERING

Number each cell. Without numbers, usually placed in the lower left corner or typed directly onto the narrow white guide band (if the transparency has one), ordering the cells is difficult. Number each cell in sequence.

TITLE CELL

First slide is a title slide. First cell is a title cell. The title cell serves the same purpose. It gives your audience a point of focus and lets them adjust their senses to the audiovisual aspects of the presentation. Always use a title cell and thirty seconds of opening comments before presenting the first important fact.

TEXT ON SCREEN

Overhead projectors are used by educators as an aid in teaching reading. This is not the purpose of the overhead projector in a meeting. Yet most users seem to believe it is. That's the only possible explanation for having the words shown on the screen exactly the same as the words spoken by the presenter. If the person making the presentation merely reads the copy on each cell, the entire purpose of the visual aid is dispelled.

It is true a recitation of the exact verbiage shown on the screen does attack two of the senses at the same time. But it is so dull and tedious the attention of the audience wanders and wavers. Many participants will read faster than the presenter speaks and reach the end of the cell copy long before the presenter is ready to change transparencies. This leaves them no alternative but to think of other subjects or mindlessly wait until the cell is switched.

Material on the screen is for the benefit of the audience, not the presenter. Many use the overhead like a TV station teleprompter. Some blissfully read exactly what is projected and do not know their material well. If a cell came out of order, they would probably read on through, taking no notice.

Written material on the screen is for the viewers. It is not a guide to the presenter. It is a way to deliver certain points and conclusions in a powerful manner and help the audience retain the desired information. Learn this lesson, or you, too, will join the ranks of those who have dutifully managed to bore people silly.

Text projected onto the screen highlights the spoken presentation being delivered by the presenter. If there are key numbers vital to the argument, these should be on the screen. If there is a graph or equation, show that. If there are a series of points which lead to a conclusion, use the overhead to list the points as they are made, then state the conclusion. For example:

Cell 1 Reduced indebtedness

Cell 2 Reduced indebtedness
        Increased profitability

Cell 3 Reduced indebtedness
        Increased profitability
        Improved morale

Cell 4 Reduced indebtedness
        Increased profitability
        Improved morale
        Higher employee retention

Four cells make four points. Each time the cell is changed, another point appears, and the previous points remain, which reinforces those previous points through repetition.

The presenter never says, "reduced indebtedness." The presenter states "improved profits in the fourth quarter allowed funding for expansion without recourse to lenders, as well as payment of certain notes which had come due." The result was "reduced indebtedness." The cell reflects a summation of the remarks, reinforces those remarks, and helps the audience understand the presentation by summing up a series of remarks as they are made. If we know the context of a conversation, we are able to make better sense of what someone is trying to explain. The overhead cell offers the context of a series of remarks.

BE VISUAL

Just as with slides, try to show interactions, needs, goals, and so on, in a visual fashion. This does not mean borrowed interest. That's as bad with an overhead presentation as one made with slides.

Be visual where you can. If text is used, it will normally be black letters on a white background. Add a little color. In the preceding example of four cells, each of which repeats the previous point and adds another point, underline the new point in yellow or place a red arrow beside it, indicating it is new. Remember, though, if you can't be extremely clever, be very simple. Just don't be simple minded enough to put the text of your talk, line by line, word by word, onto cells and show them as you lecture. Use visual images to strengthen your verbal comments and gain added attention.

FILM STRIPS

The film strip is essentially a strip of 35-millimeter film with individual frames of the film serving as unmounted slides. (Think of it as slide film before each frame is cut apart and bound into slide holders.) This strip of film is fed into a projector which takes its cue to advance, frame by frame, from a recorded audio source.

In the 1950s, film strip projectors took their audio from a phonograph record and the projector and turntable/tone arm were all built into a single unit. Today, the audio source is usually a cassette tape, still in combination with the projector.

Generally, strip film units are used for training. Individual students can put the proper audio cassette and film strip into a machine and view it for personal teaching. Occasionally, though, the film strip unit is used for meeting presentations.

Advantages are those for the slide projector. Plus elaborate audio effects are possible, including big bands, on-site sound bites, etc. Also, the film strip is a set-it- and-it-runs-itself presentation. The audio track triggers film frame change as specified in the script. And the frames always follow in exact sequence because they are joined as a single piece of film.

Drawbacks are the expense of making a 35-millimeter strip film and recording audio tapes which make this system worthwhile.

Strip film is fading from wide use, being replaced for instructional purposes by videotape recording, which offers almost equal image quality and sound, with the enhancement of movement or motion.

For meetings and presentations at meetings, skip the film strip system. Slides provide an equal image at less cost. And you can manually change slides at appropriate times as a prerecorded audio tape plays. Or, with a little added electronic equipment, have automatic, on cue, slide advancement.

MOTION PICTURES

Sight, sound, color, all are available from the slide presentation. Add the need for full-range, lifelike movement, and motion picture film becomes practical.

Movies are a specialized type of communication which use an agreed upon language to express certain conventional concepts and create action. Music behind an actor walking down a dark street begins to build in intensity and volume. The viewer knows something is about to occur. And the tone of the music indicates it will not be good for the hero.

A scene ends by slowly dissolving into another scene, and the viewer understands, without prompting, that the dissolve indicated a passage of time.

Movies have a language. It is impossible to write for motion pictures without knowing that language. So it requires a specialist to write for motion pictures. Unless that's your job, leave it to the experts.

Your involvement with the movie-making process in terms of meetings, will be limited. Note the word "meetings;" it is plural because it costs a great deal of money to produce even the simplest motion picture. And this high cost of production must generally be absorbed by multiple showings of the film.

If you get the job of monitoring a motion picture production program, to produce, say, a film for a national sales conference which will also be used in regional motivational sessions, your primary task will be to ensure that the points management wishes to make in the film are, indeed, made. You must rely on the professionals to make those points. The professionals need to rely on you to clearly state the points in simple, jargonless terms they can comprehend.

Showing motion picture films in a meeting is a more likely contact with this AV technique. If you plan on showing a movie, have the room in a proper arrangement, have a projector of the correct type on hand, and by all means, have a screen. Motion picture image quality degrades in direct relation to the projection surface. And a screen is the best.

Motion picture projectors do not produce undue heat, so there is no need to adjust the temperature for this factor, but remember that the room will be rather dark (much darker than for slowing slides or using and overhead projector) so there might be a tendency to doze.

Motion picture projectors are available in 8, 16, and 35-millimeters, to match film sizes. They are not interchangeable. You cannot show an 8-millimeter film on a 16-millimeter projector.

Once the size of film is determined, there are two alternatives: silent film or sound film.

Silent film is made without an attached soundtrack. It may be shown on a sound projector with the sound unit turned off. It is exactly as the name implies, a silent film. Even without sound, the footage may be of great value. Animals filmed in real time in their native habitat, operations in space, certain medical procedures, dynamic testing of material, and other action events in which sound has no role, are all examples of modern use of silent film.

Sound film may only be shown on a sound projector.

Quick tips: Motion picture bulbs are very hot. Don't depend on being able to change bulbs during a meeting. If the presentation is important, have a second projector which can be used in case of failure of the first. If the meeting is important, have a second copy of the film, as well, because what can go wrong, sooner or later, will go wrong.

Keystoning is a difficulty with motion picture projection, too. So do not tilt the projector to extreme angles to fill the screen. Raise or lower the whole unit.

The same comments about lenses as made under slide projectors apply here. There are more lenses, however, because with movies, most prefer to fill the screen from edge to edge at any projection distance. Also, focusing is done by hand, but once in focus, motion picture images are quite stable and remain in focus.

Motion picture projectors are becoming more difficult to locate in many companies, as the film medium is replaced by electronic recording. Motion pictures, and the photographic process, still, however, have a place. The color is superior, the effect of movement outstanding, and images are not as hard-edged as those done on videotape. The motion picture film is still the most powerful way to show a full-color action sequence to a large group of people.

VIDEOTAPE

If recording images and sound on magnetic tape does not produce as warm and striking a picture as motion picture film's photographic process, and if videotapes cannot be shown with equal clarity and brilliance as film on large screens, then why bother with videotape?

Because it is simpler to produce videotape, less expensive to produce videotape, and the time required from beginning of production to completed presentation is shorter.

You will probably never be in charge of producing a videotape recording (VTR), but the comments made for motion picture production apply.

PRESENTING VIDEOTAPES IN MEETINGS

To show a videotape in a meeting, you require the tape, a tape player, and a video screen coupled to the player.

There are many sizes of tape, ranging from one-half inch to two inches. The most common in general distribution, like the tapes rented by video stores, is one-half inch. In business, many companies have set up their own video centers. These generally use one-inch-wide tape, because of the vast variety of editing and production capabilities available in the one-inch format.

The tape-size problem is exacerbated by the fact that in half-inch tape, there are two separate recording systems. Each is incompatible with the other. So if you are to show half-inch VHS tape, you must have a half-inch VHS playback machine. If the half-inch format is Beta, the player must be of that configuration. Either format uses a standard TV set to show the picture, so there is no difficulty on that score.

About 10 people can watch a TV screen comfortably. In some surroundings, that number can be as high as 15 or 20, but crowding will occur. So if you have a large group, or are using TV presentations at large meetings, the room must be designed to accommodate additional TV receivers which can then be placed strategically throughout the meeting hall. Each receiver, usually called a "monitor," is attached to the same source for video signal by a cable. This results in wires being strung across the floor. These must be taped or run under rugs, or otherwise kept from tripping people. This is a serious danger. Especially in a dimly lit room.

One videotape player or player-recorder, like the standard home unit, can feed a signal to several monitors. And with some electronic boosting, one video "source" is sufficient for even the largest rooms.

In an effort to overcome the problems of group showings, video manufacturers have made a number of "large screen" projector units. These provide an immense increase in viewing area as compared to the standard cathode ray tube, but at noted sacrifice in clarity and brightness. Projector televisions, which have good resolution and brightness, may be rented, but these units are made for special commercial usage and are quite expensive to buy and install.

The "regular" projector model works well and is often used to provide TV pictures for thirty or forty people, with the same capability of placing multiple units in a large hall to offer several picture sites, thus servicing an even greater number of viewers.

Remember that the image is being projected onto a curved screen from a television receiver. This means lower room lighting levels (the dimmer the better, so the projected picture won't "scatter" between the receiving unit and the screen) than normally used for slides, or about that needed for a motion picture.

There is an exact and crucial distance between the projection-receiver and the screen. Some models have the two (screen and projector) physically joined together, to relieve this problem. If the two components are separate, then great set up care is needed, and may be a task requiring trained technicians. Not only does the projector have to be a specific distance from the screen, it also must be aligned in an exact plane with the screen. Again, the physically connected models care for this, albeit at some trade-off in final screen size.

The audience's viewing angle is also critical. A position too far to the right or left edge of the screen results in a dim, distorted, soft-focus effect.

In groups of a 100 or 150, half a dozen large cathode-ray-tube monitors provide the best combination of picture brightness, room light level, sharp focus, and ease of installation. The picture may not be as dramatic in size as would be produced from a larger-screen model, but ease of set up, dependability, and overall picture quality far exceed most available projector units.

While on the subject of television, the industry, which is relatively new, has produced innovation after innovation. The latest of these is called High Resolution Television. Without going into technical details, pictures are immensely better than those currently available from even the most expensive sets. High Resolution TV may correct the problems of projector to screen (large screen) units and give outstanding images, marking even further replacement of the motion picture as the standard for clarity.

OVERVIEW AND SUMMARY

Proper use of audiovisual techniques will enhance any presentation. A poor audiovisual presentation can be worse than none at all, and has been shown to actually retard learning rates and hamper clear presentation of a concept.

Using the equipment properly begins with the choice of audiovisual aid. And it is an aid, not an end in itself.

Based on the material you wish to show, select between the five options. Then create a presentation which visually holds the viewer's attention. Remember that those viewers are interested in the subject matter you are presenting, so there is no need for an extravaganza unless you are attempting to sell or motivate as well as present concepts and facts. If you can't be creative, be simple. Never be cute. Avoid borrowed interest. And last, but far from least, present your program in the shortest comfortable time.

One final thought is summed up in an old adage for public speakers: You know the concepts which you are presenting. You know the facts which support those concepts. Your audience does not. When moving a meeting toward a point, you must pace yourself with those who are slowest to comprehend your message. As the saying goes: Tell them what you are going to say, say it, and then tell them what you just said.

One of the best uses of audiovisual aids is taking the boredom out of this necessary repetition.

14 | Electronic Meetings

If it were possible to travel at nearly the speed of light, you could, in a single day, meet with managers in London, Rio de Janeiro, Cairo, and Stockholm, spend time preparing for each meeting, then be home for dinner at a reasonable hour. That sounds like an impossible schedule, because we can't travel at light speed. Yet, executives are holding those meetings, all on the same day, and never going far from their offices. While our bodies resist transport through space, our, voices and our images, carried by electronic impulses, encircle the globe in seconds, allowing us to personally communicate with others in virtually every place on earth.

This new age of global electronic communications has opened the need for learning a new series of meeting skills. The electronic meeting is not only a reality, it's an everyday occurrence.

Before we discuss proper techniques for participating in an electronic meeting, we need to consider several points dealing with definitions, limitations, difficulties, and opportunities afforded by this quickly growing phenomenon.

DEFINITIONS

There are two types of electronic meetings in which participants offer views in a personal exchange.

The first is the *teleconference*. This was once referred to as a "conference call" and has been around for decades. The advent of computers and facsimile transmission machines added new dimensions to the conference call and brought it to the level of electronic meeting.

In a typical teleconference, managers at different sites go to their offices or an electronic conference center at a predetermined time. A standard telephone call is placed to participating managers, and the group is joined into a single circuit so each can speak with the others. Many large companies maintain permanent communications channels, via land lines and satellite, so linking calls is simplified.

In the course of the meeting, all participants have access to facsimile machines so documents may be transmitted, and often a computer link is also used to allow for rapid transmission of electronic mail, special programs needed for the meeting, or reams of data to be discussed.

The *videoconference*, our second electronic meeting method, works much the same way, but utilizes television cameras so participants may see each other in action and present visual materials to the group. The fax machine and computer are also used, and common practice is to have two television channels in place so executives may watch a presentation on one screen and view themselves, the others, or any one individual, on the other. Videoconferencing is an updated, higher technology version of the teleconference. Both are singular advances over the old "conference call."

Facsimile machines do not require any special definition as they are common enough to be in many private homes. Image resolution is more than adequate, and the ability to send documents along with voice or voice and picture enhances an electronic meeting immeasurably.

Electronic mail and computers which have been crosslinked with other computers add dimension to what is possible in an electronic meeting. The computer screen of even a small portable unit can display material under discussion, and that material may be manipulated simultaneously in every terminal, which almost makes this device another class of visual aid.

GROWING NEED AND POPULARITY

With this new technology, and planned future advances, electronic meetings are increasing in number daily. Organizations are finding the techniques practical for shorter geographical distances, so even those with intrastate and sometimes innercity needs are beginning to participate.

Most managers feel the electronic meeting is not as effective or productive as face-to-face encounters, but there are growing numbers who have learned the new extensions of old meeting skills and find this system adds to their ability to manage effectively.

Upper management appreciates the lower costs, personal contact, and lessened demands upon their time which are now possible through electronic conferencing. And this means further, rapid growth of what was once an esoteric occurrence.

EFFECTIVENESS

An electronic meeting can be as effective as a face-to-face, all-in-the-same-room session. It is different and must be approached differently, but effectiveness is not diminished if proper techniques are used. Personal satisfaction, the emotional feeling after a good meeting, is harder to obtain, but with experience in this new medium, it is abundantly available.

Understanding the proper techniques, as well as how to apply what you know about face-to-face meetings, will make you comfortable in this high-tech situation. In many organizations, electronic meeting skills will be a prerequisite to promotion into executive ranks. Other organizations, not yet utilizing this business function, might well appreciate an introduction to this field from one of their own managers, because in addition to huge savings of time, there is also a sizable savings of money.

ACTUAL COST OF MEETING

In the opening chapter, there was an indication of the true cost of meeting. If participants in a meeting, which will last two hours, must travel five hours to reach the meeting site, spend the night, meet, then rush-return to their home bases, the organization has effectively lost their time for a day and a half, if not two days. And the managers have to spend a night on the road, away from families or familiar environment. So they don't return to their main jobs rested and ready.

There's no way to calculate the cost of such meetings. For less than the price of their airfares, not to mention the cost of hotel accommodations, meals, and expenses, a company can hold two meetings with the same staff, accomplish as much, and save management time for other projects.

The appeal of electronic meetings, then, is lowered cost, improved manager productivity because of more time to spend managing as opposed to traveling, and easier scheduling.

These realities will force organizations to use the electronic meeting, and that in turn will require managers to become effective in the techniques needed to express their opinions and take positions.

TELECONFERENCING

Do not think of teleconferencing as talking on the telephone. This is a meeting. In many ways, it's exactly like meetings you attend every day. Each of the participants may be in a different country, different state, different city, or in different parts of the same city, but all are together, in one place, thanks to the electronic link.

A STATE OF MIND

Picture that one place. In your mind, see it as a large room, the most ideal room imaginable for a meeting. Then put yourself into that room and populate it with the other participants. That's the right frame of reference for a successful teleconference. You've created a situation in which you can excel.

Picture another place. It's an average meeting room with one long table. Instead of chairs, rows of telephone booths are arranged along either side of the table. When you step into one of those booths, you are physically isolated from all other participants in the meeting. The only way you can communicate is through the telephone in the booth. This is not the right frame of mind for a teleconference. This is not a situation in which anyone can excel. Understand the difference?

Successful electronic conferencing, especially teleconferencing, depends on a state of mind. If participants view themselves as being in isolation booths and limited in their means of communications, the meeting has failed before it begins.

If participants see themselves as part of a real conference, able to communicate on a number of levels, the session is well on its way to success. The first task is to adjust the mind to the teleconference environment.

TELECONFERENCE TECHNIQUES

Remember the ideal meeting room? That's the right image. To support that image, you need to revise a few of your meeting techniques and make some new communications habits. Nothing drastic is required. The subject is adjustment, to apply what you know of effective meeting skills to another milieu.

HEADSETS

The telephone is the biggest barrier, psychologically as well as physically, to becoming comfortable in a teleconference environment. But without the telephone, there isn't any communication, right? Wrong. Communications use telephone lines into your office or the electronic conference area in your organization. The instrument, referred to as the telephone, is only one device to translate electronic pulses into signals your senses can understand. Untie yourself from the standard telephone. Good teleconferencing technique begins with a lightweight headset, consisting of one or two hearing units and a tiny microphone so you can talk with others.

Some teleconference rooms have built-in speakers and are acoustically designed so that no matter which way you face, if you sit or stand, a microphone picks up your voice clearly. This setup is grand, but not necessary. A good, light, comfortable-to-wear headset is adequate. It's the simplest way you can become at ease in this new environment.

The headset should be attached to the telephone unit with a long cord, so you are not tied to a chair. If you need to pace, you are free to do so. If you want to walk over and watch material arrive on the fax machine, you can. A headset removes the physical barrier imposed by the need to hold a telephone receiver.

A headset, if fitted properly, becomes almost unnoticeable in moments. Once you try it, you'll find an astonishing change in your ability to communicate over telephone circuits. The headset allows you one other luxury which restores more normal verbal communications. Your hands are free, both of them, to make notes, gesture while speaking, and do any of the multitude of other tasks made difficult or impossible because of holding a telephone.

VOICE CONTROL

The microphone on better-quality headsets is far superior to the mouthpiece on a normal telephone. The micro-mike can be located a fixed distance from your mouth, and the unit will remain parallel, or at the angle you determine, to your lips regardless of how you move your head. This means the volume of your voice is fully controllable by how loud you desire to speak. Your full dynamic range, from above a whisper to just below a shout, will be transmitted as you create. So instead of having to accommodate your voice volume to the instrument, the device allows you to react and speak normally.

Experience shows that participants in teleconferences perform better if they slow their speech speed. This doesn't imply dragging words or using prolonged pauses. It merely means to talk as you would under relaxed conditions. No need to be more careful of word pronunciation. If people can understand your usual speech, the new microphones, with their improved dynamic range, will deliver your voice well enough to ensure comprehension.

Speaking too slowly can be a drawback because no one can see your face so there is no visual cue as to your intent. Speaking too slowly can therefore be mistaken for demonstration of any of a number of negative attitudes toward other conferees.

Speak deliberately. Just as you would in a social environment where you are relaxed. Let your voice volume rise and fall with your feelings, as you world normally. There is less disturbance in a teleconference than in many regular meetings because the tendency towards ever-increasing volume, as one person strives to be heard over the voice of another, is absent.

VOICE TIMBRE

Don't try to pitch your voice differently. Some feel a deeper tone on the telephone indicates more presence and control. That may be true, but inconsistency in tone destroys your telephone identity. The ability of other participants to recognize you depends upon their ability to recognize your voice. As you shift from the lower tone, which is not natural, to a higher one, which is your normal sound, your identity will change, and that's not good for making your points.

If you must have a lower, more resonant telephone voice, take appropriate voice training. Perhaps simpler is looking into the purchase of an electronic "filter" which will produce the desired effect. Really, though, both these actions are extreme. There is no need to be anyone but yourself. The closer you can stay to your own identity, the better. Falseness eventually shows.

SPEAKER IDENTITY

You have your headset on, there are seven other managers included in the conference circuit, and someone speaks. Who is it? From the voice, it's a woman, so it can't be Sam or Randy or Bob. But is it Alice or Brenda? Not knowing who is speaking affects how you perceive the message. It's like sitting in a regular meeting blindfolded, trying to guess who is making what point. That is bound to impact your judgement.

In teleconferencing, there are a number of means to the valuable end of knowing who is speaking. Here are a couple tried, tested, and proven techniques.

Identify yourself at the start of every speech you make and, if appropriate, address your remarks to one or more of the other participants by name. For example:

Tom: . . . and so, I don't think we can make that deadline and not go over budget.

Mary: Tom? Mary. We've got to find a way. There isn't any more money. And we need it that day.

Mary identifies herself at the beginning of her remarks. Everyone knows who is speaking. She addresses her remarks to Tom, the previous speaker. Addressing Tom helps focus her need and appeal. He has made the statement which requires probing. He is the manager to be addressed.

If Mary had come on the line and said, "We've got to find a way . . . ," Tom might be confused as to who was speaking. And Mary wouldn't have the correct focus for her comments. In her own mind, she might know she was talking to Tom, but to the group, her comment would seem to be a somewhat meaningless appeal—a restatement of what all already knew.

This demonstrates an interesting psychological point about communicating in a teleconference: Face-to-face, we direct our remarks, usually without reference to names, by eye contact. Others can see the object of our attention, thus clearly perceive our meaning and intent. Not so in the teleconference. Words spoken without designating who is specifically being addressed are considered to be spoken to the group.

To repeat, because your understanding of this point is crucial to your ability to teleconference well, a remark addressed to a single person has different meaning and weight than a remark to the group.

In the example, Mary is making an appeal to Tom. She is saying the task must be accomplished on schedule with no further expenditure of funds. This comment, made to Tom, states Mary's position and asks him to work with her.

If Mary had simply said, "This is Mary. We've got to find a way . . . ," her statements, because they are made to no one person, would have been taken by some members of the group to be a vapid generalization, not focused on the problem. The difference is important.

So in addition to identifying yourself at the beginning each time you speak, also identify, if your remarks are aimed at one person, to whom you are speaking. This must be done in a conversational manner, instead of the formal fashion of an airport-tower operator or police-radio dispatcher.

"Tom? Mary," is better than "Tom, this is Mary." The longer "this is" form is fine for the beginning of a meeting, but switch as soon as possible.

Regrettably, there will be participants in teleconferences who haven't learned the trick of identifying themselves or the individuals to whom their comments are made. Do not hesitate to break into someone's speech to ask, "Who is this?" or "Who is speaking, please?" during the early parts of a meeting when dealing with people you do not know or haven't frequently been telelinked with or haven't heard speak for some time.

Each speaker should identify him or herself, and if addressing another participant, identify that individual. For example:

Mary: Tom? Mary. I believe . . .

Tom: Tom. That's fine, Mary, but it doesn't change . . .

Mary: Mary. I know, Tom, but . . .

Tom: In any case . . .

You should state your identity, unless you are certain the others know who you are. The name of the party you are addressing can be used naturally in conversation, or as an opening salutation.

Once the exchange between two people begins, it is no longer necessary to continually identify yourself and the person you are addressing. The others are following your conversation and know who is speaking. Be as natural as possible in the use of names, but use them. Both yours and the person you address.

A MEMORY AID TO IDENTIFYING SPEAKERS

Remember imagining the ideal conference room to get yourself into the right frame of mind for a teleconference? That same technique can help you identify participant's voices.

Make small table-tent cards, like the placecards used to put names in front of faces in a regular, all-in-the- same-room meeting. Align them on your desk or work surface in the teleconference center. If you know any of the people, print a few key words of physical description beside the name. If there is any special quality in a voice, such as a regional accent or unique speech pattern, note that, too.

When you talk to another participant, look at that person's card. You can go so far as to try and imagine the person's face, but that's not necessary. Just associating the person with his or her card and its notes will instantly help you relate to that individual and learn the voice.

HAND GESTURES

When you speak, help yourself speak normally by using the same hand gestures you would talking to someone face to face. Using gestures will relax your voice and make your speaking more effective. Don't be self-conscious. Use your hands the way you normally would. That's one of the reasons you are wearing a headset—to free your hands.

LISTEN

If it is important to listen in face-to-face meetings, then the need to listen in telemeetings cannot be overstressed. Remember: The telephone only takes one of your senses, that of hearing, but you still have to receive and retain the message with the same alacrity, as if all your senses were in play. Face-to-face, you use vision and hearing, and, probably, although psychologists are not in agreement on this, smell. Sometimes, there is even physical contact, adding touch. That's a great deal more sense input than merely hearing another's voice. Yet you are expected to understand and retain, so you can contribute and help reach a decision.

In teleconferencing, you add your own extra sense stimulation to improve your learning-retention abilities. This is done by making notes. There is no need to take down every word, but there is demonstrable need to make clear notes on who is saying what, to help you follow the group's action. You hear it, you think it, you write it, and you see it. That's closer to the same level of sense stimulation you would experience in a face-to-face meeting. And it's little trouble to do. Your hands are free, thanks to the headset, so note taking isn't an added chore.

Note taking can be another way to learn voices and know who is speaking.

List the first names of each participant at the top of several sheets of paper or on multiple pages of a pad. As you take notes, refer to the names, depending upon who is speaking, and also indicate in your notes who says what. For example:

Mary	Lou	Glen	Scott
Tom	Roger	Gloria	Barbara

Tom: Can't make budget deadline.
Mary: Must.

This system works well, allows you to know who to address before you speak, and re-enforces the names of participants as you hear their voices.

Note taking is mandatory for the group leader. There is no other way to control the direction of the discussion, determine who is and is not participating, discover if one or two participants are dominating the conversation, and so on. Memory is not sufficiently refined to monitor the volume of information needed by the leader to maintain productivity of a meeting.

Leaders take notes. There is no other way to lead a telephone conference.

THE LEADER'S ROLE

Teleconferences must have a leader. The leader must fulfill the role customary in face-to-face meetings and also moderate exchanges among participants in the teleconference. The moderating effect is needed to keep everyone from talking at one time or to prevent an exchange between two individuals continuing until the meeting is dominated.

The leader makes an opening statement, exactly as in a face-to-face session, then starts the discussion by calling on one participant to begin. For example:

Leader: . . . so our need is great and our budget short. Or almost nonexistent. Everyone understand our problem?

Group: [General agreement.]

Leader: Okay. Tom, your bunch has to build it. Without altering your other delivery schedules. Where are you on this?

Note that the leader has to listen. First, when asking if everyone understands the problem. It is not necessary to call roll, but the leader must stay alert for insufficient or weak response from participants. This indicates the problem is not fully understood by all.

The question to Tom, opening the discussion, isn't casual. Before the session, the leader decided on a line of attack; in this case, to pursue the problem from the standpoint of manufacturing. It could as well have been opened from the views of those controlling the money or the deadline. In any case, discussion would begin from a given point which leads into other possible solutions. The same specific-view technique is often used in opening face-to-face meetings. It is far more important to begin telemeetings in this manner, because the single-track approach makes it easier for a leader to maintain direction of the discussion.

LEADER AS MODERATOR

Mary responds to Tom with an appeal. Tom rejects the appeal, sticking to his position, i.e., the task cannot be accomplished. If allowed, the two will talk each other into silence before either will submit.

The leader must recognize imminent deadlock, which stops all conversation, then act to minimize the exchange between Mary and Tom before they meet mutual frustration. Bringing others into the discussion in hope of finding a compromise for the two positions is a good technique.

Teleconferences tend to produce positions quicker than face-to-face encounters. Positions are often espoused in response to the first question. Also, because each participant is alone and not under the scrutiny of others across the table, positions are not quite so solid when they are taken. However, positions can quickly become irreconcilable.

In moderating between Tom and Mary, the leader must step in before they become frustratingly intransigent. If care isn't taken, the two will speak only to each other, which after all is how we normally use telephone circuits, and ignore the rest of the group. This happens in face-to-face meetings, too. It's just more pronounced over the telephone.

The leader has several ways to control or moderate the group. One of the best is to have a few more opening questions. For example:

Tom:	So there is just no way...
Mary:	[Interrupts.] But there has to be. We...
Tom:	I tell you there isn't...
Leader:	Tom, Tom?
Tom:	Yes?
Leader:	Excuse me. You and Mary seem to be deadlocked. Let's go at this another way. Barbara, what's the real financial limit?

This direction change is effective. It brings in new minds, gives Tom and Mary time to leave the ground they were defending to think of another approach, and opens the door to fresh participation. If Mary insists on responding to Barbara, the leader should break off that contact. Both because Mary is still emotionally confronting Tom and because she is dominating the conversation, lessening the others' opportunity to participate.

Another technique is to use the fax machine. If the leader does not want to appear to be interfering, he or she may interrupt to say, "Mary? Tom? Hold it a second, will you? There is a report, showing progress to date, and funds expended to date, coming in on everyone's fax. That'll give us some hard facts to . . . "

The leader has sidetracked the argument and has not indicated from whence the fax transmission is being made. In truth, the leader may be the one making it. The arrival of real numbers, even though many in the meeting may already know them, allows the leader to throw the matter to another participant, by calling attention to some aspect of the financial figures.

Both techniques require adequate leader preparation. More preparation than may be needed for a face-to-face conference. But much less time required than it would take to gather the group and hold an in-person discussion.

PACE

The meeting's pace is another leader responsibility.

It is possible in a face-to-face session to have exchanges between participants so rapid that no one, even the person being addressed, can respond. The exchange slips into a babble of voices, all talking at once. Confusion happens even more frequently in teleconferencing. And can be prevented, to a large part, by regulating the discussion's pace.

"Pace" is the rate of exchange, the speed with which complete thoughts may be expressed and understood. If the exchange becomes too fast for the leader to take accurate notes, the leader should break in and slow the pace. Just as it is imperative to speak a little more slowly than normal, it is equally important to have the flow of ideas, discussion, and so on, delivered at a slower rate than normal. It isn't because participants are any less quick to comprehend. It's because fewer senses are being stimulated and, if all are note taking as any leader hopes will be the case, getting the second and third sense-registrations through the medium of handwritten notes takes a finite amount of time.

Pace is also a control against everyone's speaking at once, which can happen easily in teleconferencing. Especially when discussions are held by inexperienced teleconferencers.

Once the pace has quickened, the leader usually cannot stop further increases without direct action. Breaking into the conversation with a few remarks, delivering them slowly, helps, but isn't as effective and is more time consuming than interrupting and telling everyone to slow down because you, the leader, can't make notes fast enough. If, as leader, you make it your inability to keep up with the speed of discussion, no one feels blame and all are more likely to assist in maintaining pace.

THE MEETING MANDATE

Do not enter into a teleconference without knowing what you want to accomplish. The old rule, still true, even in this age of electronics.

Managers tend to be more casual about teleconference preparation. Don't be guilty of this error. If anything, teleconferences take more preparation, because you also need to focus on recognizing the others in the meeting. So your mental effort used in presenting your position is shared with this identity difficulty. The old Scouting motto: "Be prepared" was never more true than for the teleconference.

ALLIANCES

In teleconferencing, alliances are more easily detected than in face-to-face meetings. Not being able to see the participants actually seems to help when trying to sort out who is joining whom, or how factions are aligned. Leaders of these factions are more easily recognized, too, as the others tend to hold back and let the leader speak. With no facial expressions or body language to distract, it's much easier to recognize a leader's tone.

HOLDING TO THE SUBJECT

Keeping the conversation on correct course and ensuring that participants hold to the proper subject is simpler, too. The leader must listen, but variations from the subject are easily detected. A good leader breaks in quickly, though, because once a deviance starts, it will grow quickly. Again, digression seems to be caused by only feeding one sense. Note taking helps limit the discussion to the topic under consideration.

TRANSLATIONS

With teleconferencing able to span such large distances, it is only natural that, sooner or later, a language barrier will occur. Which means dealing with simultaneous translation.

In situations where great exactness is required, say in negotiation over a contract with many specific clauses, all work must be reduced to writing. Discussion concerns the written proposal. In such instances, nuances of language can cause misunderstandings. To prevent variances, both sides should use the double translation system.

The document you create in English is translated into Italian by translator number one. Translator number two then takes the Italian version and brings it back to English, which you then compare with your original draft. Retranslation allows you to spot problem sentences or words, work out a solution with the team of interpreters, and produce a final document which means the same in both languages. The agreement is then faxed to the other parties, in both languages, and your meeting can begin.

There is a temptation to trust interpreters, especially good ones. Just remember that we are all human, possessed of a tendency to avoid offending others and slow to bring bad news to our leaders. Translators often attempt to soften the edge of a hard stance or blunt the point of a sharp remark. Both acts make negotiation more difficult, because it becomes impossible for the negotiators to judge the other's desires or intent.

Translators double the number of individuals in a teleconference. If three individuals are involved in talks and each brings a translator, suddenly there are six. Which means more margin for error. One cure for this is to let the translators handle the telephones. You tell your translator what you want to say, your message is translated, delivered, and a response comes back over the circuit.

See anything wrong with this? Seems simple enough, but in this system, you never get to hear the voice of what the English call your "opposite number." If you are not going to hear his or her voice, don't bother with the telephone connection in the first place. Use a computer network to send screens back and forth until the deal is agreed upon. You need to hear the other person's voice. Even if you do not understand a word of the language, hearing the voice brings you closer. For this reason, both you and your translator need headsets. A "kill" switch is helpful, so you can talk with your translator and not have your words satellited toward the other parties.

Translation slows the meeting process enormously. So much, in fact, that an agenda for such a meeting should only have one or two items. A discussion which might take 10 minutes with all participants speaking the same language can take 45 minutes to an hour. So keep the meetings simple, limit the number of topics, and hold more sessions. It may take longer, but more will be accomplished.

Some electronic conference areas have provisions for instant translation services, like those used in the United Nations. Through an earphone, you hear the speaker's voice and the translator's interpretation. This kind of installation isn't common yet in this country, but as need increases, there will be more such facilities.

When being translated, speak a sentence, pause, and let the translator translate and transmit. Talk to the translator as if he or she is the party you are addressing. Speaking directly gives you an opportunity to express emotion on your end and have at least some of it reach the other person. The translator will respond to this and it will affect the choice of words and tone. When the translator speaks to you, encourage the same technique. He or she should speak to you as spoken to, trying to convey some of the emotion from the other end.

Multilanguage teleconferencing, where three or more languages are spoken, places demands on the translators which are so great that the opportunity for error is drastically increased. View these situations with concern and do not rely on them for sensitive negotiation.

SPEAKERPHONES

Electronic conference areas often use a type of speaker telephone where any one of a group can talk and all on the other end of the connection can hear through a common instrument. These are fine and easy to work with, providing the room is acoustically correct to prevent hollowness or echo. In meetings where two groups, or three groups, in different locations, come together electronically, the speakerphone allows fast participation. And users tend to forget the rules concerning identifying themselves and the individual to whom they are addressing their remarks.

Be careful with speakerphone-type instruments. Do the necessary identification work when offering your comments. Don't let the group atmosphere generated by the device lead you into believing everyone recognizes who you are.

One speakerphone plus: Used by a small group in the same room, the electronic conferencer doesn't feel as isolated. There is more of a sense of participation, which can help the meeting's productivity.

There is one drawback, too. It is hard to beat the clarity of sending and receiving attained by the headset. And experience indicates some people have more difficulty listening when speakerphones are employed.

THE FAX MACHINE

Of our many electronic marvels, this little dandy has to be ranked high on the all-time list of great aids to long-distance communications.

The only problem is that most managers don't understand how to use this wonder to get the most out of a telemeeting.

Think of the fax machine as a visual aid—a kind of overhead projector. Transmission time is longer than it takes to change a cell on the projector, but the end result is a sheet of paper in everyone's hands, which can turn into a participatory experience.

The presenter introduces his or her subject. There is no title slide, of course, but the introduction allows transmission time for the first document which may be thought of as a cell. Only instead of the information being displayed on a screen, it is on paper, in front of each participant. As soon as the first document is sent, the presenter begins transmitting the second, while still discussing the first. During discussion of the second sheet, the third is put on the wire. And so on.

Copy on each "cell" needs to be a little more elaborate than for overhead use, but the general idea is the same. You transmit a summary of important points, along with backup facts, and leave participants with a complete, albeit brief, presentation of your position.

Adding a participant-sharing feature makes this technique even more effective by forcing multisense exposure to your important points. This can be done in a number of ways. Here is an example:

The fax machine is delivering the first page of the presentation as the speaker completes introductory remarks.

". . . so in addition to there being a serious time problem to meet deadlines, we also have strong financial constraints. Please look at the document on your fax machine. It's a two-part illustration. On the top half, there is a graph, which shows normal production rates and days required, at those rates, to attain the number of units we need. See the point marked 'A'? The one the arrow points to? That's where manufacturing costs begin to decline.

"Now look down below. At the second chart. That's the reverse of the first, based on manufacturing costs and volume. There's a point 'B,' on that one. Got it?" [Presenter waits for positive response before continuing.]

"Now the two points are . . ."

This is an effective presentation. It took some imagination to develop a form for information which would allow other participants to become involved with the data, but a second sense has now been added to the mix.

In teleconferencing, the fax machine is more than just a convenient way to deliver documents. It is a practical, effective device to enhance presentations and drive home crucial points. Be imaginative. Follow the rules for slide and overhead projector presentation, modified to allow all participants to handle the slide or cell themselves. Get participants into the presentation by having them mark points on a graph, circle figures, underline dates, and so on. It's interactive and effective.

It is a good idea to put your name and home city on every sheet you fax for presentation. This helps identify you and your material while making plagiarism a little more trouble.

COMPUTER SCREENS AND PRINTOUTS

What can be done with a fax can also be done with computers. Interlinked desktop units allow grand presentation possibilities. With everyone watching the same "screen," numbers can be manipulated, special portions of a document can be enlarged and highlighted, graphs may be produced, tilted, reflected, elongated, or otherwise manipulated, and other dynamic visual effects are possible to give your presentation more impact. And all this takes place in real time, in front of the participant. With the addition of a computer screen projector, a readily available accessory which projects a computer screen's image onto a wall, an entire roomful of people can view your presentation simultaneously. If you're not a computer expert, or even novice, counsel with someone who is and try to find ways to use this dramatic tool. Computers and electronic meetings go together well.

ONE LAST COMPUTER TECHNIQUE

By mail, supply all participants with a disk compatible with their desktop computers. Once a telephone circuit is made, ask each participant to load the disk and key along with you as you talk. Your presentation is on the disk and no interconnection is needed between computers. This technique may take a little time to develop, but the effect is quite stunning. Hard-copy computer printouts, allowing later consideration of material, add to the effectiveness. Remember to include your name and city on each sheet just as you did with the faxed material. Identification helps prevent many problems.

SCHEDULING ELECTRONIC MEETINGS

Scheduling face-to-face sessions may be difficult; scheduling electronic meetings can be a real challenge. First, consider the difference in time zones. Be considerate. If you are calling the meeting, do it at the most convenient (normal business hours) time for the majority of participants. If anyone has to get out of bed at 4:00 A.M., make it you. The others will appreciate it.

Another obstacle comes from business customs. Lunch is common through most of the world. What is not so common is the meaning of that word. In Italy, it might be a three-hour afternoon session with drinks and a large meal. In Japan, it may be a 20-minute, grab-a-bowl-of-noodles-in-the-company-commissary,-eat,-and-get-back-to-the-drawing-board. Remember your working day isn't that of the rest of the world.

On top of customs and time zones, add the other common meeting scheduling difficulties, and it's easy to see there can be problems. No hints here beyond those already offered for scheduling face-to-face sessions except a reminder that everyone's calendar is subject to rapid change. So don't rely on the postal service to set meetings. It's far too slow.

And like face-to-face sessions, it's easier to get all to agree on a next date when they are in the same room. Which electronically means at the end of the meeting you just completed.

TAPE RECORDING

Many electronic meetings are tape recorded from beginning to end. This is good and bad.

On the good side, such a record allows you or any other participant to replay the session and determine exactly what was said. Or how something was said. A leader can use the recording as a check on meeting control and a learning tool for improving group performance.

On the negative side, the action of tape recording squelches some managers' ability to participate as fully as they might. And the act of tape recording, knowing every comment has the potential of being evaluated later, tends to stifle offerings of unusual solutions or novel concepts, for fear of later reactions.

Deciding to record depends on your need for a detailed, contemporaneous record. For negotiations, it could be a lifesaver. For situations where translators are used, it might well be a wise tactic. In other instances, though, taping can kill imaginative input.

Remember this: If you are recording a session, make sure everyone knows the session is being recorded. Expect this same courtesy from others. There are privacy laws and big trouble can come from violations.

If the meeting is recorded, everyone should get a dub of the tape. That's common electronic courtesy.

AGENDA/MINUTES/MEETINGS MEMOS/MEETING FILE

A meeting is a meeting whether electronic or face-to-face. The same concepts about agendas, minutes, meeting memos, and your meeting file still apply. If it is difficult to hold a productive meeting with everyone in the same room without an agenda, it is far more difficult to do this in an electronic conference. Stay with the principles that work. Deserting them will not result in better electronic meetings. The result of shortcuts in these areas is chaos.

Have an agenda and stick to it. Have that agenda distributed, by computer or fax, prior to the electronic session.

Create minutes, review them, and make sure everyone gets a copy.

Use the meeting-memo technique. Mail, or if time does not permit, fax them. Memos work especially well in this electronic situation.

Your meeting file is even more important. Maintain it. If the group meets regularly and will do so for an extended period, send photos of yourself to the others and request their pictures. Or send a camera around and ask for candid shots. Or use computer imaging. Getting a face attached to a name helps.

VIDEOCONFERENCES

What has been said for the more common teleconference also applies to video meetings. But some emphasis changes are needed and there are a few techniques just for the sight-sound-motion medium.

SLOW PACE

The advice on slowing yourself for teleconferencing is also true for video meeting. This needs to be driven home to every participant. When it's audio alone, speak more slowly. When video is added, move more slowly. Be deliberate, not stiff. Be relaxed and alert, but move a

tiny bit slower than normal. Again, do not exaggerate this. Control
your movements, especially quick arm motions. They come across
the screen wilder than in real life because video pictures have a hard
edge. They are immediate, with sharp colors, and tend to enhance
motion. Do not become a slow loris or three-toed tree sloth in movement, but do slow a little. The best word seems to be "deliberate."

PASSIVE VIDEOCONFERENCE

Video sessions can be divided into two types of meetings. One, the
passive mode, consists of an individual appearing live, on screen, before groups of managers in one or more locations. In many ways, this is
a lecture or presentation, usually given by an upper echelon executive.
There may be some interaction between the person on screen and the
audience, or there may not. In fact, the performance of the presenter
may well have been videotaped, to edit for time, remove problems, and
generally enhance the presentation. In this case, the participants are
watching what amounts to a TV program.

In passive meetings, interaction comes through taking questions
by telephone, or having cameras in the receiving locations, and re-
questing response from the viewers. Remember that the entire presentation, including questions, may be on tape. So the appearance of live
participation may only be illusionary.

Passive meetings can be quite effective, are growing in use to
perform sales training or product-training, and can bring an organization's rank and file in touch with top management.

The passive meeting is a developing technique.

ACTIVE MEETINGS

Active video meetings take place in real time, except as noted
below. Active meetings feature face-to-face discussion and group decision making. Videotape recordings may play a role in these meetings,
say for presentations, but the brunt of the session is a live exchange
of views.

A passive meeting is sometimes combined with an active meeting
by showing a presentation (passive) featuring the organization's president, which has been prerecorded, then moving from that taped event
to an active mode, conferring to frame decisions necessitated by the
president's appeal.

For purposes of this book, the active meeting is more important than the passive, although there will be a brief discussion of the passive conference in the chapter on large meetings.

The active session is, in every sense, a true meeting. It is normally conducted like a meeting, attendees prepare as if attending a face-to-face meeting, and business decisions are made. Normal meeting skills are used and normal agendas, minutes, meeting memos, and meeting files are developed and applied as usual.

SENSE STIMULATION

Video meetings are face-to-face encounters. Each participant sees and hears the other participants. The difference is presence—Physical presence, or the lack of it, and working in what at first is a strange environment.

VIDEOCONFERENCE CENTER

You may hold a teleconference in your own office, but it's unlikely you will be involved in a video meeting outside a properly-equipped television studio. It takes a great amount of equipment to send and receive pictures and even more to add the special effects which replicate a meeting environment.

Videoconference centers, also called electronic meeting areas, provide a number of discrete functions. A quick run through will familiarize you with essentials.

First, there is the meeting room. When it's to be used for a teleconference, it becomes a stage set. A teleconference room is pre-planned to handle from one to many (usually up to twenty) participants at the same time. A table of sufficient size is generally available. If a more informal atmosphere is desired, the set may be a single armchair. Or a replica of a full-size boardroom. In any case, the set area is planned to be acoustically correct. Baffles, which remain out of view in the various camera angles, and soundproofing, provide a quiet, echo-free area in which even the roar from air-conditioning vents has been removed. It's a restful space, conducive to relaxed thought and contemplation. Your normal speaking voice sounds louder in this area of quiet.

The "set," in addition to providing acoustical control, confines your zone of activity. This isn't to stifle you but to allow close monitoring of three functions: sound, lights, and the picture to be transmitted.

Microphones, either hidden, clipped to your clothing, on overhead booms, or in plain sight on a table, pick up your every word. As well as every sniffle, snurf, throat clearing, and every other nonspeech noise humans make.

The set has been constructed so you don't have to face in a particular direction to be heard perfectly. In some sets, a small body mike is placed under your shirt or clipped to your lapel. This is an additional sound source designed to provide even greater freedom.

Lighting on the set gives sufficient illumination to allow the TV cameras, which are quite small, to develop an excellent electronic picture. At the same time, the lighting sweeps away sharp contrasts between bright and dark, banishes shadows, and gives a feeling of depth in the final transmitted image. The TV cameras optically scan this area of enhanced lighting to electronically produce images as real as life itself.

Excited electrons, carrying your every word, are fed to a central source, where they are recombined with their cousins, which remember your picture, and together they flow through an engineering process to produce a balanced, synchronous television presentation with the proper mix of sight and sound. This engineering center controls the microphones and cameras on the set, then further adjusts what they deliver into a final audiovisual image. Once in this state, the "picture" is sent, as a stream of electronic impulses, to a transmitter, which strengthens the signal and relays it to other sites, where participants await your presence. Transmission may be through the air, to a satellite where it is bounced back to earth, through wires linking your site to microwave relay towers, or any combination, including telephone lines.

At the same time all this is occurring, another part of the videoconference center is receiving signals from all other sites linked for your meeting and processing those signals into pictures and sound so you can see and hear the other participants.

All this sounds complicated because it is. The marvel, though, is the simplicity of the equipment in terms of operation and size. Which introduces a caveat. If you are placed in charge of selecting a videoconference center for your organization, do not be led astray by hardware. The best, latest, most sophisticated gear is no better than the people who operate it. Laundry lists of technical capabilities and black boxes are no substitute for trained, experienced, dedicated men and women who know television. People, as with most human endeavors, make the difference.

Videoconference centers are increasing in number. A large motion picture chain in the East has several theaters in different cities equipped to offer teleconferencing on an hourly basis. A top U.S. insurance and financial company has built its own teleconference center. And many other organizations have such centers completed or in the planning stages. Teleconferencing is quickly leaving the novelty stage and becoming an everyday occurrence for many executives. In the next few years, television meetings will play an important role in American business, commerce, and government. This is a good time to begin honing the special skills needed to utilize this new meeting style.

PERSONAL HINTS

Automated cameras, better transmission techniques, and the new high-resolution TV all combine to improve picture and sound quality. Which means the other participants in videoconference will see you better than ever before. And you will see them. Next is a quick primmer on how to look your best and perform to your top capacity.

ISOLATED IMAGE

When you watch television, you see an isolated image. It is a picture, isolated from its surroundings, formed by a glowing tube contained in a box. In that isolated picture, you see what the camera sees. And what the camera sees is not what the human eye sees.

When you look at someone across a conference table, you do not see him or her in isolation. Your focus is on that person, but you are aware of background, foreground, and peripherally, everything in a field of vision which covers nearly 180-degrees. That isn't the same as the isolated view a camera delivers.

The isolated camera view is like a square chopped out of the full picture you see. And because it is a portion of the normal human view, it is enhanced by its being singled out or separated. This is an important concept, because it explains what all TV performers know and many business executives must learn. The television picture is, in its own way, bigger than life. It is an exaggeration, because of its isolation. And to exaggerate in an already exaggerated situation is to appear awkward and probably foolish. Remember: When on the TV tube, all except a narrow wedge of background is gone. The focus is on you. If you exaggerate, your overstatement will be noticed by all. Probably not favorably.

SLOWER AND SMALLER

On TV, go a little slower—just a bit, but slower. Slower in speech and slower in movement. Remember, others can see you in a teleconference. A sudden turn of your head, the necktwisting, shoulder-raising used to relieve a muscle, abrupt large arm movements, are all motions which would go unnoticed in a face-to-face situation. On television, where you and your movements are magnified, your peers will notice. And you won't look your best.

Slow speech. Don't drag it out, but slow down. Be deliberate. Move more slowly, using less grand gestures. Think slower and smaller.

VOICE

Refer to the comments made in the section on teleconferencing. Your natural tone is best. Stay with your natural voice. The studio team can help deepen or lighten your tone by microphones on the set. If you like, let them but speak in your normal voice. Don't exaggerate.

MAKEUP

A properly lit set, with you in it, produces the best picture. But the best picture may not be your best presentation. Removal of shadows from your face and the set around you requires lighting that is far more intense than that found in a normal room. It's closer to the illumination on a bright summer day. Only this light is not as "natural" as sunlight, which comes from one direction and produces shadows. Set lighting comes from a multitude of directions and tends to wash or lighten skin colors. Set lighting also enhances that which shadows help hide. Light complexioned men with dark facial hair can look unshaved even after shaving. Darker complexioned women can appear to have circles under their eyes.

The answer to all this is makeup. It's the only answer. Not the everyday makeup or even the kind worn on stage by actors, but the right type makeup, applied properly to enhance your TV appearance. Use of the wrong makeup is worse than none at all. The correct makeup restores what is distorted and lost due to lights. Unless you want to look distorted and lost, wear makeup. Let an experienced TV makeup artist show you how to apply it, then watch your audition tape.

AUDITION

Before your first video meeting, you need a quick on-camera "audition." You go on the set for a few minutes, let the technical staff videotape you, then watch the replay. You'll learn more about makeup and dress and movements and mannerisms in three minutes than you can any other way. Let a makeup specialist see the tape and teach you how to make yourself look better. Don't be afraid to wear makeup on TV. Not much is used and the results are worth it.

CLOTHING

On your audition tape, wear what you feel is appropriate conference clothing. Then watch for these common faults.

Men

1. Coat gapes at the back of the neck when you lean forward.
2. Shoulders look too padded when you raise your arm(s).
3. Shirt color (white) contrasts too greatly with the dark color of your suit or the light color of your tie.
4. Tie does not fit properly into the inverted "V" of your collar.

These are the four most usual glitches in men's appearance on TV. Cures are simpler than visiting a tailor.

When you take your seat on the set, adjust your coat by rolling your shoulders forward and tugging lightly, away from your body on your lapels. Then sit back and look at yourself on the monitor to make minor adjustments. Your shoulders won't look too padded if you don't raise your arms. And there is no reason to raise your arms. Make your gestures tight and talk with your hands, as you normally do at a conference table. Watch out for contrasting colors. Blue is a good color for a shirt to wear on TV. It's softer and doesn't register on camera as a harsh contrast. Shiny material should be avoided, that includes shiny ties. And if your tie-collar combination can't be made to look right, change to a thinner-material tie. That usually helps the problem.

Women

1. Colors contrast sharply.
2. Jewelry, including pins, lockets, rings, big shiny belt buckles (and shiny belts), earrings, and hair adornments can cause

reflections, which are usually seen as unattractive black, irregular blotches.

3. Lustrous silks or synthetics cause reflective problems.

4. Tight-fitting clothes, especially those which cling to the upper torso, can look rather revealing at some angles under TV lighting. A tight fit can also make you appear overly plump.

5. Sheer fabrics which can be penetrated by light will often produce embarrassing images on the TV screen.

The general female rule is to dress for an executive meeting, staying within the customs of your organization, and play down jewelry. Even a wristwatch on a bare wrist (men's shirts and coats cover their watches) can cause reflections.

Both men and women should understand that it can get hot on a set under the lights, even in spite of added air conditioning. So dress accordingly. And a couple of off-white handkerchiefs or a small towel, to blot a sweaty brow when not on camera, can add to your comfort. Heat isn't the problem today it was in the past, but it can combine with the strain of the meeting to produce perspiration.

HAIR

Do not develop a TV hairstyle. Be yourself, which is difficult enough under the circumstances. Changing hairstyles alters personalities in many people. Balding men get a small break on TV. Your makeup master can help if you are concerned about receding hairline. The technique doesn't stop hair loss and won't work under normal lighting, but is fine on the tube.

MICROPHONES

Microphones are not selective. The set is wired for sound pickup and that's what happens. Sounds are picked up. All sounds. Including those you'd rather not amplify. Beware of unruly noises, from drumming your foot against a table leg to popping knuckles to grunts and other biological or psychological response sounds. Be careful about laughter. All microphones have a resonant frequency, and laughter, from giggles to gales, often is amplified and becomes much louder or sharper.

CAMERA TECHNIQUE

Talk to the camera and make eye contact with the lens. Then you'll be looking into the eyes of the other participants. If you watch the others on the TV monitor, which will be in your line of sight, you'll appear to be gazing fixedly into space. Remember that viewers only see what the camera shows.

Be reasonable about eye contact with the camera. Make contact as you begin your remarks, then relax, and if you look away, as you would in normal conversation, it will appear normal. Especially if you talk as though you were addressing one person.

Addressing remarks to a group produces strange reactions because you are looking at the camera, so looking, as far as each individual viewer is concerned, into his or her eyes. Which is a signal of personal communication. If your remarks are too group-oriented, they won't match the intimate visual signals. Hence the advice to attempt to keep your comments to one person.

MONITORS

Ideally, you will have a monitor, or TV receiver, within easy line of sight. Sound can come from the monitor or through a headset or from speakers in the videoconference room. If you are videoconferencing with a group, and that group is being covered by two cameras, then it's helpful to have a monitor for each camera. One will usually be shooting the entire assembly while the other is trained on the speaker. This gives a better feeling of group reaction and allows you to gauge your remarks.

AUDIOVISUAL PRESENTATIONS

A videoconference is one big AV presentation in and of itself. The fax machine allows for interaction, just as it can in a telemeeting. Ditto the computer. It is possible to show a slide presentation, complete with your voice or recorded sound, an overhead presentation, or even a strip film, but best results will come from pre-taping your presentation, using TV techniques. This allows you to edit and improve, and at the same time hone your presentation skills by watching yourself in action. Don't be afraid to do this. There is little or no loss in spontaneity. With one exception. There are presentations designed to have participants ask questions as the presenter offers his or her views. If that's the case, do it live. Just be sure the technical team knows what you are going to do and there is an area on the set prepared for this purpose.

In videoconferencing, assume your every word is being recorded on videotape, because it probably is. Taping is often done as part of the transmission function, to protect against signal loss. Many times, the taped record is erased almost as soon as it is made. Other times, tapes are filed, for study by engineering to learn how to improve the video signal. And in still other instances, the tape is required by organizational policy.

Recording meetings can have the same negative effects on spontaneous contributions as in teleconferences. Participants in videomeetings must simply resign themselves to this and learn to work around any resulting psychological barriers.

TIME DELAYS

An electronic signal, traveling from earth to the moon and back takes a finite time to make its journey. This is evidenced by the pauses during communications with astronauts participating in the American lunar landings. Add to this delay the microseconds needed to pass the signal through transmitters to boost it into space, and the time lag grows.

Using some satellite systems, what you say in the videomeeting won't arrive at your other participant's sites the instant you say it. There is a lag. You don't notice it while speaking, but in give-and-take exchanges, it becomes a problem, because the flow of conversation is disturbed.

There is only one cure for this difficulty, and that is to slow speech even more. Listen, and when you are certain the other party has stopped talking, then you can begin. Slowly.

The time-delay factor in most videomeetings is not large enough to attract attention. Just don't be surprised when it happens. It can be an unsettling experience.

PRACTICE

All videomeeting participants become more effective after a few hours of conferencing. One technique to shorten acclimation time is to practice. Most videoconferencing centers welcome managers who would like to develop their video skills. Group leaders will find a few hours spent in practice will make them more comfortable. As mentioned earlier, watching yourself on videotape is an excellent learning experience with benefits for face-to-face meetings as well.

Electronic conferencing has grown in a few years from a business novelty to a regular, routine activity for many executives. The benefits of a well-conducted electronic meeting are the same as for a face-to-face session. And costs are much lower. Managers who take time now to add this skill to their professional inventories will find long- term career benefits. Many managers who enter into this field today will assist in their organization's entry into the world of electronic meetings.

15 | The Large Meeting (Super-Meeting)

Many organizations periodically hold really large meetings where many hundreds of attendees gather in a central location for discussions, presentations, seminars, recognition ceremonies, training, and other activities. The organization holding such a conclave is usually responsible for providing accommodations, meals, entertainment, space for various meetings, and direction for the group. Managers assigned to create and conduct these super-meetings often feel intimidated and helpless. With good reason, because mega-meetings are complex events. But like most complicated projects, they can be broken into simple, manageable components. Which makes planning and conducting the session a less formidable assignment.

This chapter reviews several types of events and offers guidance in conducting and controlling them.

PAST MEETINGS

History is your first guide. Review of past meetings can show which activities were most beneficial or popular, which did the most to attain the meeting's goals, how controversial ideas can best be presented to attendees, and a multitude of other important facts.

If your organization has held previous meetings of the scale under discussion, there are, it is hoped, records of those super-meetings.

If so, consider yourself lucky because most super-meetings are held but never rehashed, condemning those in charge of the next session to repeat their predecessor's mistakes. If you are involved in planning or conducting a super-session, your assignment is not ended until you have prepared an after-meeting report.

AFTER-MEETING REPORT

It may seem odd to begin a discussion of super-meetings by bringing up the after-meeting report, but that's where all large sessions should begin. By discovering what worked in previous years.

If this is the first super-meeting your firm has ever conducted, there will not, of course, be any reports. In this case, you are no worse off than many firms which have held them for years but never bothered to keep or require after-meeting reports from the organizers. If you have such reports, use the experience to make your super-meeting better. If there are no reports, use your best judgment and see to it there is a full report on your session.

MANAGEMENT INPUT

The first formal step in planning a super-meeting is to confer with top operating and executive officers of your organization. Planning work is impossible before this necessary session, because planning a super-meeting cannot begin until goals have been defined and broad budgets established.

If the event is an annual affair, arm yourself with two items prior to the top management session.

1. *Budget.* Review records and determine what was spent for the last super-meeting. This question is sure to arise. If you can, learn the authorized budget for that big meeting as well. You may be encroaching on dangerous territory if a previous manager exceeded the budget but kept that fact from the top executives. Be tactful when revealing actual cost information.

2. *Goals.* Define the goals for the previous year's event, then estimate how well those goals were met. Some will have been attained better than others. This is information management needs to make decisions on this year's affair.

If this is your organization's first event, or if there are no records, try to get some idea of the cost of other firms' large sessions. Call travel agents, professional meeting-planning groups, friends at other organizations which hold such affairs, and hotel meeting-sales managers. Sort through their knowledge. Think your way through and suggest those goals which seem possible to accomplish. Remember that for super-meetings you are probably planning a year or two ahead of the actual date.

In this first meeting, you need agreement on the goals of the super-session and a dollar amount which you may use as a basis for planning. You are not seeking approval of a budget or expenditure. You want guidance. You need to be aware of top management's attitude towards the super-meeting and understand what they wish to accomplish.

If at all possible, set deadlines for the completion of an overall plan, a total budget, and selection of a site. With these deadlines, arrange follow-up meetings with the highest ranking executives who will be involved in the decision-making process. These upper echelon men and women have busy schedules and may be frequent travelers. Thank them in advance for their participation.

SUPER-MEETING PLAN

The super-meeting plan consists of a number of elements. The proposal must be in writing, state goals, assign responsibilities, have deadlines, and serve as the overall guide to the affair. The following is an outline for developing such a program.

1. *Description of the Event.* Use a paragraph, or a page, as necessary. A typical description might read:
   "The Enomeek Corporation's 19th Annual Jamboree. This is our annual new-products meeting where our dealers and sales staff are introduced to the latest items in our line. This three-day affair offers several business-oriented sessions, a golf tournament, a tennis tournament, a fitness/wellness program, shopping, three seated dinners, including the annual President's Award Presentation Banquet, and a dealer-improvement seminar. Time will be provided for interaction between top management and our dealers."
   The event description capsulizes the meeting. It is not a place for statement of goals. Think of it as a description to a dealer your organization wishes to have attend. It should sound

interesting, exciting, and worthwhile. The event description is what will happen. Not why. That's the goal's prerogative.

2. *Goals of the Event.* This is why your organization is spending its money. The true purpose of the mega-meeting. If the goals are not well defined, do not anticipate a good meeting. Miracles happen, but not often enough to award such misplaced anticipation.

EXAMPLE: Goals

a. *Attendance.* To get 70 percent of our dealers from the following retail areas to attend.

   (1) Dallas/Ft. Worth

   (2) Omaha

b. *Sales.* To allow John Ramet, Executive VP, Marketing, to meet with and evaluate dealers from the Midwest and East Coast.

   These goals are not ephemeral. They are not: "To build rapport with our dealers," or "to discover new relationships between the sales staff and dealers," or "to enhance dealer-management fellowship."

   The goals offered by management in the initial meeting may be general or couched in less direct terms, but the manager who is planning the super-meeting must be specific.

   Goals fall into many categories, including attendance. (How many of which attendees are desired, any special—by name—individuals whose presence is a "must"; which staff members will be on hand, etc. Being specific prevents misunderstandings later, so delineate attendance in some detail.)

   Other goal categories might include the exact opinion your organization wants its dealers to have concerning a new product, particular relationships specified sales people are to develop, changes in your organization's image, etc. Goals must be specific enough so that after the meeting, in the post-mortem report, you can list each goal and detail its degree of attainment.

   If you cannot list a goal specifically, you don't understand it well enough to accomplish it. And if you don't fully understand a goal, there is little chance of reaching it. Specific goal descriptions will appeal to management, too. Objectives are a gauge to guide progress and evaluate the success of the session.

The most common error in plans for super-meetings is ill-defined goals. Start with sharp, definitive, specific goals and your program will come together with ease. Start with too general or poorly-detailed goals and your program will never be effective. Define your goals as specifically as possible.

3. *Preliminary Budget.* Present the money before discussion of activities. Don't take the attitude this plan is a selling document. In a sales presentation, money always comes after statements to create need and value. In this plan, the cost must be related to the goals, so management is given information in this order.

If you have records of past super-meetings, judging the budget will be simple. You know what was spent last time, can add factors for inflation and any meeting format changes, and have a good "ball-park" figure.

Without those records, budgeting is a bit more time-consuming, but the results are probably better.

Meetings may be broken into several components for costing. These include:

a. *Travel*

b. *Accommodations*

c. *Food and beverage*

d. *Entertainment*

e. *On-site transportation*

f. *Meeting rooms and service*

g. *AV equipment*

h. *Awards and prizes*

i. *Special events*

j. *Guest appearances*

k. *Special insurance*

Other categories may be added to suit your needs. Division of expenditures into categories forces the meeting planner to evaluate the price of each activity and its benefit.

The travel expense includes your organization's contribution, which typically will range from one hundred percent to no contribution at all, for transporting all attendees, including your own personnel, to and from the meeting site. Work with an airline representative or travel agent. There are tables which give a general idea of this expense without recourse to listing every flight for 800 different individuals coming from a variety of cities.

Be aware that travel costs for many of your managers and sales people may have already been included in the sales or marketing budget. This is especially true if the super-meeting is an annual event.

The balance of the categories may be dealt with by contacting a travel agent, the selected hotel, or a professional meeting-planner firm.

In any event, add a generous contingency, as budgeting at this stage is not sufficiently comprehensive to cover every detail. And some prices will change over the months which elapse between planning and the session. Note that while the budget is presented in this slot, it cannot be developed until all other considerations are resolved.

4. *Site Selection.* This can be fun or absolute agony. And the difference depends on your attitude. The site is important because it affects attendance, costs, and event activities. People enjoy certain cities in America, or overseas for that matter, more than others, so are more likely to attend a super-meeting in a preferred city, especially if they are paying their own way. Also, some cities offer to help arrange group discounts which, add to their desirability.

Travel costs to certain cities will also influence site decisions. Some very popular locations are more expensive to reach from certain areas of the United States. If those areas contain individuals on your must-attend list, this ought to be considered.

Upper management will also influence site selection. As will site availability. Super-meeting plans are frequently made years in advance so reservations may be secured in premium hotels.

One system for site selection is to make a list of possible locations by calling a travel agent or the hotels directly. A hotel sales agent can give you full details on accommodations, available dates, competing meetings (Super-meetings do compete. And collide. There are only so many golf courses and large banquet rooms. If a number of major groups are in the same town at the same time, capacity stress may affect use of all facilities and weaken service.), competing costs, and other factors. In fact, the hotel sales staff can be your best friend in conducting a successful conference.

Once a listing of available sites is complete, investigate transportation rates (airline sales agents, travel agent, meeting planner), and other criteria as determined by past meetings and/or the original meeting description. Narrow your list to three or four choices and gain management approval. Then place your body on premises to review facilities and negotiate. This is time-consuming, but worth it. You'll be treated very well and may be able, by personal on-site negotiation, to save your organization a considerable amount of money on room rates, banquet expense, etc.

Narrow options to two locations and refer the matter to the highest level of management available. Make a recommendation, if you like, but let the upper echelon decide, so you can tell people later that the site was "their" choice. Why set up this excuse? Necessity. With so many different personalities involved, someone, at some time, is going to say to you, "I just do not understand why we are going to (went to, or are at)" wherever. They are going to be irate when they say it and may even be on the verge of becoming irrational. To be able to invoke the authority of upper management at such a time will make life easier for you. Do not, at risk to your personal safety, bypass this final approval step. The site-selection segment of your plan must have deadlines. And specific assignments if more than one individual is to conduct site inspections.

5. *Invitation List and Proposed Total Number of Attendees.* Every plan should include as complete an invitation list as possible. The list should have the name, home address, and telephone number of each invitee known at the time of writing the plan and should be amended or expanded as meeting arrangements progress.

At times, it is not possible to generate such a list because many attendees will register during the final months prior to the session. Make your list as complete as you can, including members of your own organization, then estimate the total number of people who will attend. Recall that an attendance figure is a goal, listed among the goals in part one of the plan. An accurate attendee list, begun early and frequently updated, will serve as your guide to attainment of that goal and allow you to encourage the sales or marketing staff to contact and recontact key customers and other individuals whose attendance is required to reach the stated goal.

Regardless of the type of event, some form of registration through a central office, with copies to you or your staff, is mandatory. You must monitor progress towards the attendance objective. The attendance segment of the plan specifies how this is to be done and actions to be taken if goal achievement appears slow.

6. *Special Transportation Arrangements.* Many organizations use chartered aircraft. Some rent railroad cars. Others hire express buses. If your activities include any form of special transport, enumerate it in detail in this section. Do not forget insurance arrangements, if needed. Also included in this section are special arrangements to pay transportation costs for entertainers, guests of honor, honorees, sales contest winners, award recipients, and so on.

7. *Activities.* Another requirement is a complete listing of each activity, framed into a daily schedule, which shows there is time to do all that is planned. An additional, separate description of each activity relates it to a special goal. Plan no activity that cannot be related to a goal. If a golf tournament is traditional, find a way to orient it to attaining one or more goals. If your general sales manager needs to meet three dealers, and that meeting is listed as a specific objective, then the golf tournament is an ideal place to do so. If they all four play the game.

Do nothing and plan nothing which does not have goal attainment at its heart. Just because there has always been a golf tournament is no reason to continue having one. The golf tournament must fulfil a stated goal or assist fulfilment of one or more stated goals. Holding it because the chief of your organization has a long-standing bet with a top marketing executive is foolish.

More money is wasted in super-meetings because managers fail to relate specific goals to events than in any other way. Goal attainment is the reason for holding the session. Goal attainment is the justification for spending a considerable amount of money. The meeting's events are crucially related to goal attainment. So the events are important. Every minute of them. And must be planned with the aims in mind.

Many managers are inclined to argue this point and seek exception. There is no exception. Including the activities planned for the families of attendees. If there is an event or activity, there must be a goal or goals which that event or activity helps attain. Period. No variances. No excuses.

Each event will be the responsibility of a manager within your organization. Name this manager. Be certain that person knows the goal or goals to be accomplished.

8. *Go/No-Go Attendee Requirement.* Bad timing, an economic downswing, an industry-wide condition which upsets production or profits, all these and more are specters haunting the manager responsible for planning and conducting a super-meeting. It is often difficult, projecting a year or more ahead, to foresee dire events which directly affect the success of your super-session. The only answer is to press on regardless to a "go/no-go" point. The go/no-go date should be part of every contract and agreement. Management should be aware of this date and agree it is the point of no return. If the decision is to go, to meet, then the meeting will be held. If scaling down is indicated, this should be provided for as a contingency. If cancellation is indicated then cancel at this time.

Acts of God do occur. And some can completely disrupt a super-meeting. No preplanning is sufficient to cope with all contingencies. So the go/no-go date system is as good as any for seeking final approval.

9. *Disaster Plan.* There is a fire at one of your plants. An airliner crashes and several in your organization perish. Food poisoning strikes after the president's banquet. Disaster and threat of disaster, including bomb warnings, are part of our business environment. So every super-meeting must have a disaster plan. This makes provisions for responding to the press, dealing with attendees, evacuation of all or a portion of those in attendance, special communications within your organization, etc. The plan should be brief. Specify by name who is authorized to speak with the press, note exactly what approvals are required for press and other information releases, and, again by name, delineate which manager is in charge of each event scheduled for the session.

Making a disaster plan is not pleasant. Implementing it is even less so. Neither unpleasantness is akin to the confusion and harm to your organization which can occur if such a plan is needed but is not part of your master planning.

Other categories may be added to the master plan, as demanded by your particular meeting's requirements. The above outline provides sufficient insight into the structure of such a plan and the considerations which drive the planning to allow you freedom to complete a written outline covering your specific needs.

HELP SOURCES

Get help with the plan if you feel it is required. Sources include travel agents, meeting planners, hotel sales staffs, airline marketing staffs, those in your organization with past experience in this field, your advertising agency, etc. There is a wealth of experience and information which can be yours for the asking. So ask.

SPECIAL CONSIDERATIONS

Super-meetings are unique events, and as such have a number of considerations which occur only with this kind of activity.

Here are some insights into several areas of concern:

1. *Internal Sales Meetings.* Many organizations gather their dealers and sales teams into a super-meeting then hold a special session for the sales group. Avoid this. Let your sales team do its job during the meeting by visiting with their customers as opposed to spending time with each other or their management. Hold your sales meeting before or after the customers arrive or depart. While customers are present, let your sales group do what they do best. Sell.

2. *Transportation Facts.* America has been inadvertently sectioned by airline service and tariffs. Some desirable cities are not so desirable, in terms of transportation costs, if travelers come from both coasts and the Midwest. When evaluating locations, get sample airfares from cities spread across the United States. Ten or so should be enough to show the effect of rate problems. There is no indication the dividing process has been deliberate, but as manager in charge of a super-meeting, you need to be aware of its existence and the impact on rates and time required to reach certain destinations from certain points of origin.

3. *Hotel Evaluation.* Trained hotel marketing people know how to answer questions in a way which is beneficial to their property.

As in every field, there is a jargon. Work through this, so you are certain both you and the hotel marketer are speaking the same language. (Hotel people are not the only ones with jargon. Travel agents speak a their own brand, as do many convention meeting planners.)

You need to know if there are sufficient rooms to accommodate your group, if there is enough "public space" to allow areas for meetings and banquet setup at the same time, depending on your activity schedule, and the quality of the kitchen. If your group requires display space for exhibits or space where suppliers show their wares in a trade-fair environment, include these needs in your original request for information.

Get a response in writing, then speak with the head of the hotel's marketing team. Request a formal proposal after the initial weeding-out process. Hotel marketers are busy, and while glad to make presentations, appreciate not being asked to do so unless their property is on your approved list.

4. *Travel Agents.* Travel agents can provide valuable assistance. Especially in the early planning stages where the encyclopedic knowledge of some agents is invaluable. Travel agents can also simplify making travel arrangements, ticket delivery, etc. You will pay for their service. Understand this, and if you use an agent, ask for all the service for which you are paying. Travel agents can do many things to ease your chief executive's trip. Or get VIP treatment for selected customers. Some agents say going through their system and using their services doesn't cost any more than buying tickets directly from the common carrier. In some cases, this is true. In other instances, it isn't. If you are transporting a quantity of people to and from a meeting site, there are ways to cut costs. Some travel agents know these. Some do not. Some of the agents who know how to cut costs wait, before offering the cost-saving tips, to see if you will ask. Those who ask shall receive. It's an old rule. So ask. And ask an airline sales representative too. The two-bid system is great. You can compare direct costs as well as special services. And know what various special services actually cost.

5. *Hotel Staff.* All hotels handling large group sessions have a trained staff to help your team with the necessities of check-in, checkout, luggage transportation, changing accommodations, and the myriad of other details which arise when a few

hundred people arrive for an overnight stay. Hotel staffs are efficient, effective, and have dealt with almost any problem you will encounter. Use their services. When making arrangements for your group with the hotel or resort sales management, determine how these individuals should be compensated for extra effort, and add that amount to your budget. Close relations with the hotel sales people and their service staff are assets you can draw upon when needed. Don't deplete them with minor requests. Use them freely when the cause is right.

6. *Professional Meeting Planners.* Many people make a business out of planning meetings. A few are true professionals in this field. They have the experience, knowledge, and unique skills that make them stand out and excel. The question is, how do you locate such professionals? One method is checking references. Have a couple of meeting planner-firms give you contacts with satisfied customers. Then call the contacts and discuss the services offered and services delivered. You'll get a rather good notion of the firm's ability. During your reference check, ask about individuals with the planning organization. Remember that you might be hiring a firm, but only one or two people will do most of your work. If you get the right people your experience can be as glowing as some of the references. If you don't, it doesn't mean the references were wrong. You just didn't get the same staff.

There are a number of compensation plans for meeting planners. These range from normal travel-agent commissions on all hotel and transportation, to added fees for specified services, to straight hourly charges.

Contrary to what a few of the more eager meeting-planner companies would have you believe, their services will not relieve you of the complete burden. Meeting planners will not do everything, and if they did, your meeting would not be a success, because they would not have the necessary understanding of your goals and special needs. Meeting planners can be a great help. Many do a fine job. Most are familiar with the leading resorts and hotels, with travel arrangements, and with organizing group activities.

Do not automatically opt to hire a meeting planner or avoid hiring one. Make your plan, and while arranging various parts, make contacts in this field. Check references, then talk specifically about your super-meeting needs. Base your decision on cost versus service offered. Be aware of hidden revenues when you negotiate. Be open and expect candor, especially in the area of finances, from those with whom you deal. If you hire a planner group, make them your partners.

7. *Passive Video-Sessions.* There is a growing trend towards the use of passive videoconferencing for parts of a super-meeting. The chief executive and operating officers of an organization can make specific statements to special segments of the attendee group then field questions through a real-time, active video or teleconferencing system.

   Many organizations have cut their meeting costs by holding three or even four separate meetings, each done regionally in a different city, at the same time. Top echelon management of the organization flies between meeting locations and uses videoconferencing, mostly in the passive mode, to fill in their appearances. Benefits of this system include: lower transportation costs, savings on hotels, meetings more tightly tailored to regional needs and attitudes, and lessened contact between dealers.

   The passive video-meeting will be more widely used in years to come, because it allows chief executives, whose time is limited, to appear in a number of different places and deliver a strong message. Passive or active videoconferencing is worthy of consideration as an adjunct to any meeting now in the planning stage. Just ask which goals can be met this way and consider cost savings plus availability of management for all or part of the scheduled meeting dates.

8. *Satellite Gatherings.* Another growing trend is to hold one large meeting around an official opening and an official closing event which everyone attends. Then, because the number of attendees is so huge as to be unmanageable, the group breaks into smaller components, based on regionality, interests, needs, and so on, and the mega-meeting becomes a cluster of satellite mini-meetings. All participants take part in the planned activities, both social as well as business-oriented, so there is a feeling or sense of cohesion throughout the group. Often, much more can be accomplished this way.

   The satellite-meeting can be used to a lesser degree, by having only one or two special groups split off from the main mass. If you must deal with an enormous number of people, say over a thousand, you might well consider this satellite concept.

Satellite-sessions are also held by multinational firms and organizations as a means of coping with language barriers. Combining passive videoconferencing (in which all audio, including music, is translated into each nation's language or most common tongue), with simultaneous sessions in each country, creates what is probably the most effective and inexpensive worldwide meeting. Active video enhances this even more.

9. *Entertainment and Stars.* Entertainment is an accepted part of every super-meeting. This runs the gamut from unorganized, unplanned late night card games between attendees to athletic competitions to lavish musical presentations designed especially for the conclave. All "official" entertainment must be preplanned and controlled.

Entertainment is a feature of the meeting program, so must meet the test of goal attainment. If you cannot show how each entertainment event advances the attainment of at least one goal, you have selected the wrong entertainment. On this subject, don't fall into the trap of writing a general goal, such as "to improve customer relations through fellowship and sharing common experiences." No fair. That's not a goal. That's a given for every large meeting. Don't write a goal to justify a specific entertainment. Make each entertainment justify its place on your schedule.

The hotel sales staff can handle most locally-based entertainment needs. An orchestra for a dance, for instance, or a chamber music group or Dixieland Jazz band for a brunch, or a golf tournament, are all typical, easily-met requests. Special needs, such as a magician with a vanishing act which ties into a new cleaning product that vanishes dirt, can be obtained through talent agencies in the meeting city. Just be sure to allow enough lead time.

Attractions, like a custom musical comedy with singers and dancers, or a complete circus with animals, or a pro-am tennis tournament with touring professionals, are also available. In fact, if you can conceive of an extravaganza, it can be created and produced. Albeit at some expense. Sources for this level of entertainment are regional or national. The larger talent and booking agents, headquartered in Los Angeles and New

York City, are the correct sources for exceptional presentations. One caution. If you plan an original production, deal only with the established talent management organizations and those individuals they recommend. And if a director is required, insist on seeing each prospect's past credits.

Talent management firms can also provide recognizable entertainment or sports stars who will attend your super-meeting and lend a special flair to an event. This same source will also know which stars might be in the general area of your meeting, working on location or appearing in concert, and offer you a reduced rate to "book" a convenient entertainer. At times, real bargains can be had. Check out the star first, though, to avoid embarrassment or partisanship. (Ronald Reagan, for example, was an active spokesperson for privately-owned municipal power companies. Because of this, he would have been, in his entertainer days, a questionable guest at a national meeting of publicly owned municipal power systems.) Above all, get management approval. The talent representative will be able to provide a list of commercial and charitable appearances the star has made during the past several years. Examine this critically.

And please, please remember that while stars add glamor, they must be carefully used so as not to obscure the reason for the entertainment. Or shadow your own organization's top management.

When negotiating with stars, usually done through their agent, make certain all duties expected of the star are clearly delineated. If you want the individual to sign autographs, have this in the contract. If you expect them to hand out photos, include this. Many, many heart-thumping moments, caused by a star who believed the assignment was one thing and arrived to be requested to do another, could have been avoided. Agree on specific duties, length of appearance, and terms of payment.

Entertainment and star appearances are attendance boosters. Both are costly and may consume a large portion of your overall budget. Plan carefully and make each expensive happening goal-attaining.

10. *Free Time.* Many super-meeting planners, anxious to receive the most benefit for the outlay of funds, schedule an activity at every possible opportunity, with no worry about free time for

attendees. The assumption is that anyone who wants time off will take it by simply skipping an event or two. It is better to schedule too much as opposed to too little. Attendees will take free time when they like.

11. *Pre-Meeting Preference Surveys.* There is a growing trend to survey, formally or informally, prospective attendees, in order to get their preferences for types of events, special sessions, instructional seminars, and so on. Polling is a good idea. The super-meeting event schedule is the strongest incentive for attendance. If many sessions meet the needs of attendees, there will be more attendees.

Techniques for taking these surveys vary. Two good approaches are (1) direct telephone calls to selected individuals who are on the must-attend list, to define their likes and dislikes, and (2) direct-mail polls to a broader base of potential attendees. In attempting this preference sampling, be sure each respondent is asked the same questions in the same words. This helps prevent misinterpretation of data.

There is a temptation to allow the sales force to inquire about the proposed program during research calls. This isn't a good practice. First, because personal bias is almost invariably allowed to skew respondent's answers. This bias comes from the marketer's own judgment and a tendency to select respondents with like tastes. Or a selection of respondents the sales person is interested in having present at the meeting. Second, a conversation with a customer by a sales person can place the sales person in the role of having to deliver an event at the meeting as specified by the customer, or lose face.

If a pre-meeting preference study is made, do it through an impartial survey firm or use a portion of your organization separate from the customer-contact function.

12. *Room Assignments.* One of the guaranteed horrors of a super-meeting is unleashed by room assignments. In every large session, one or more attendees will be dissatisfied with assigned rooms. Complaints are endless and show great variety. One suite will be too close to the elevators. An attendee who ordered an inexpensive room will be assigned a suite and refuse to pay such an "outlandish" rate for "just a place to sleep." Another, who wanted a suite, will receive a single room. Still another feels his or her room isn't as nice as a friend's accommodations. The list is endless.

Expect problems in this area. Have the hotel staff standing by to help. Honestly try to resolve every complaint. You won't be able to, and in fact, you'll be doing better than most if you can maintain a pleasant demeanor. Those problems that are clearly the hotel's, refer to the hotel for resolution. Those which are emotional or based on personal preferences, try to settle. It takes diplomacy and tact. And it's easier if you know you are going to face this situation. Make up your mind. You are. So protect your flanks. Explain to your top management that there will be difficulties in room assignments and some degree of dissatisfaction. Tell them you have done all that can be done to alleviate this unpleasantness. Do this before your super-meeting begins, so they will know what to expect. And can place proper perspective on being approached by an important customer who is irate over accommodations. This problem is part of a super-meeting manager's life.

13. *Security.* Boys do it, girls do it, and it's done at every super-meeting. There must be a super-network throughout the United States, because whenever there is a super-meeting, a super-number of shady and unseemly characters show up as uninvited entertainment hosts.

   You cannot monitor attendee morals. That's not your job. Who goes where with whom is a matter of individual choice. At the same time, however, attendee protection is important. If a stellar customer is robbed, or rooms are burgled during your meeting, the meeting will not be a success, at least for the injured attendees.

   Guest security is a matter for the hotel while guests are on premises. In dealing with the hotel or resort sales team, insist on meeting the head of the facility's security service. You may need help so this is an important introduction. During this session, ask about fees for added security. And about advance notice if more security is necessary. Also, depending on your group, it's not a bad idea to make prior arrangements with a bail bondsperson, just in case there is need to remove an important attendee from durance vile. The facility's security chief can usually recommend a reliable bonding source. Put this information into your disaster plan and hope you never have to use it.

14. *Doctor in the House.* You don't want to use these services, either, but just in case, meet and speak with the house physician.

If there are medical facilities on site, inspect them. Be sure there is adequate medical service available for common problems which can stem from some of the planned activities. Examples might be: pulled muscles sustained during athletic contests or sunburn because of a tropical location. Don't expect or seek a physician who can perform open-heart surgery. There are hospitals for that. You need a qualified medical practitioner experienced in handling the more common human disorders. You also need a fee schedule and hours of medical service, which can be provided by the resort or hotel.

This is more information for your disaster plan, which, again, it is hoped you'll never use.

15. *Your Team.* You've been assigned responsibility for managing a super-meeting. It's an exciting challenge. You are going to need help. The question is, how much help, when?

A typical mega-meeting takes about a year to plan. During the first six months, time is mostly internal, although site visits must be made as early as possible to make reservations. In fact, most large groups are booked two or even three years in advance, so you may already have a site when you are placed in charge. Even so, you have to make a site visit, to familiarize yourself with the property and the potential activities available.

From six months prior to a super-meeting until a full month afterwards, your time will be progressively devoted to the needs of the session. For sixty days prior to, during, and after the meeting, you will be involved in meeting business exclusively. That may sound like a lot of hours, but experience shows it isn't.

From the beginning, a year or so before the event, you will need an administrative assistant. Correspondence and filing are critical to good meeting management. Ideally, this individual will be able to keep schedules and learn the names of those with whom you are dealing, including travel agents, hotel staff, meeting planners, your advertising or sales-promotion agency, talent managers, and the like. A good administrative assistant is invaluable in handling calls or fielding problems when you are on the road.

And you will be on the road. Because of this, you will also need two additional staffers. One should be assigned to logistical considerations; travel reservations, room reservations, banquet planning, cost controls, and the like. The other should be responsible for the program and activities, taking approved goals from your plan and creating events to attain them, securing necessary talent, entertainment, and so on. The division of labor between basic program logistics and activities bearing on the conduct of the meeting is a good one. There is little overlap of duties, and as the responsible manager, you know who has which answers.

For some, with no experience in planning and conducting a meeting of super-size, a staff of four seems too small to effectively deal with a thousand or so people. In actuality, the full time of all four individuals is not required until 90 days before the event and will be needed for only two weeks afterwards. Naturally, four individuals cannot greet arrivals, fill out name tags, check guests into the facility, hand out meeting packets, and so forth. Part of this work falls on the appropriate members of your organization (sales/marketing, if the meeting is sales oriented; top management, if top customers will be present.) If a fifth person were added to the team, that individual should ideally be versed in bookkeeping and your organization's internal accounting practices.

16. *Tasks.* Individual plans made to handle the various components of the meeting, one plan each for the two different managers, should be comprehensive and created by task. Pre-meeting confirmation of attendance is a task. The "look-forward-to-seeing-you" letter from your chief executive is a task. Check-in is a task. To help, here is a general listing of tasks connected with a typical meeting.

  a. *Six Months Prior.* Meeting announcement, a selling package which gives dates, place, and events to be included in the meeting, goes to all potential attendees. Sales and marketing, as well as upper executives, receive advance copies of this packet for their use. Each packet contains an invitation, information on events, encouragement to attend, a rate sheet if required, and information on the city and hotel or resort. Mailing lists must be checked by management and approved prior to use.

  b. *Four Months Prior.* All talent and entertainment is booked and set. A meeting reminder goes to all potential attendees.

  c. *Three Months Prior.* Last-call reminder to all potential attendees who have not responded. Confirmed attendance lists are submitted to various managers in your organization to be certain critical individuals have not been missed and are receiving proper attention.

NOTE: Pre-meeting confirmation of reservations is sent on an individual basis as each reservation is received and processed.

d. *Two Months Prior.* A letter from your organization's chief officer, which in effect says, "I'm personally looking forward to seeing you at the meeting," is sent to all those who have registered. A second version of this letter goes to key individuals who have not yet agreed to attend.

e. *One Month Prior.* Conferences with hotel or resort staff and checks on all meeting rooms, banquet arrangements, and entertainment. Complete confirmation that needed personnel, either hired for the job or from your organization, will be on hand for necessary training sessions the week before the event takes place.

Final mailing to all attendees, reminding them of hotel or resort facilities, and so on. Give a telephone number (hotline) to call with questions. (Your telephones will be very busy one week prior to and during the event.)

Last attempt to get uncommitted but desirable attendees to register.

f. *Three Weeks Prior.* Begin moving your offices to the hotel or resort.

Attendee packets, consisting of necessary tickets, badges, name tags, a special list of numbers to call with questions for assistance, and so on, should be prepared. Usually one per attendee is required.

g. *Two Weeks Prior.* Second check on all entertainment and events. Confirm readiness. Any loose ends? Tie them off at this point.

h. *One Week Prior.* Move onto premises of property. All operations for the meeting will be conducted from this new headquarters. Be certain your staff knows hotel and service people, including head of security and house physician.

All attendee packets on hand with proper attendee names. (Verify names and spelling. Check VIP names twice.) All extra personnel trained in their tasks.

Have a nice session.

The above is necessarily brief and intended to outline the need for a number of items which can easily be overlooked or forgotten. It is a rough guide, not a complete checklist. Develop your own formalized checklist, with tasks for each month, and then stick with it.

Your team is important to the smooth operation of the meeting, for propping up attendee morale, for quickly solving guest problems, especially those of VIPs, and for resolving last-minute transportation, room, or reservation difficulties. You and your team must forget about 8-hour days or 40-hour weeks during the session. Consider yourselves on call 24 hours a day, every day.

17. *Pre-Inspection and Post-Inspection of Facilities.* Super-meetings go wrong because of miscommunications. Inspection of facilities prior to the event, then again afterwards, is necessary.

Placing your body on premises two to three weeks in advance, long enough to review all preparations, events, and so on, is a giant step towards sound communications. Likewise, doing the same thing a few days after the last attendee has gone can save your organization money by cleaning up problems which might have arisen during departure. The pace is much too hectic before the meeting, when attendees start to arrive, and immediately afterwards when they depart, to efficiently look after the business and financial aspects of the super-meeting. Your hands will be full. Do your business in the pre-meeting and post-meeting visits.

Ground transportation is a good item to check during pre-visitation. Be sure the taxi companies are aware of your meeting. Be certain any bus transport you have arranged is ready and has the proper schedule.

You can delegate a great deal to your staff. Bring them along, if necessary, but attend to the pre and post-visits in person.

18. *News Media.* Many super-meetings are closely followed in local, regional, and national press. This is especially true when there are public figures who speak on controversial topics. Press interest means reporters and camera people. Which in turn means a need for control. Or chaos will ensue.

Do not rely on the press to control itself. Members of the fourth estate are present to get a story and do not care about your meeting or your plans, other than as they concern that story.

Almost every super-meeting needs a press room, which is a site with ample telephones installed, an abundance of outlets for electronic word machines, access to limited refreshments (coffee, soft drinks, snacks), tables and chairs. Most press rooms also contain stacks of printed material related to the meeting and personalities attending the session.

Dealing with the press is one of the most difficult tasks in conducting a super-meeting. Not because reporters are difficult, but because, in most cases, the information your organization wants to disseminate is not the news the press is seeking.

If your company has a public relations staff, they should be included in the meeting-planning process from the beginning. Many firms entrust the meeting to the PR people and appoint a manager to oversee their efforts. Hotels also have public relations specialists who can be of service and assistance.

If you are in charge of a super-meeting, it is a good idea, if your organization has no PR function, to retain a firm specializing in this area while making the initial plan. Let these experts advise you on potential news angles and stories. Then determine if this coverage is satisfactory to management. If so, continue the relationship right through the conference. If not, replay management's desires for coverage and get an honest estimate of the possibility of gaining such press attention.

Many super-meetings choose to assume a low profile in regards to media coverage. This requires a degree of secrecy if there is a controversial figure or speaker involved. The hotel or resort is well-equipped to handle these matters. Turn to them for aid.

Determine your management's attitude towards media exposure before making your plan. Unless your upper-echelon executives are enthusiastic about making news, it's best to avoid all press activities. If there is enthusiasm, then by all means plan for active press participation.

In your conversations with management, remember that the trade press, whose work appears in magazines and newsletters published solely for those in your industry or field of operations, can be approached separately from the mass media. So it is quite possible, and often done, to hold events of interest to reporters specializing in your business without attracting writers from the general-interest media.

19. *Smaller Sessions.* Almost every mega-meeting has a series of smaller sessions scheduled throughout the conference. These may range from presentations of R&D papers to new product announcements to dealer information seminars to awards ceremonies.

The smaller, special-interest get-together has become an integral portion of the larger meeting and is, in fact, the reason many participants attend. The meeting-within-a-meeting concept is so successful that many firms offer partial registration, allowing selected individuals to attend a main event and several smaller groups as opposed to enrolling for the whole program.

If you plan to break your super-meeting into groups, see to it that a top person in your organization is present at every one of the mini-meetings. The presence of someone recognized as being an important member of your organization's management has a salubrious effect on those attending the smaller session. The presence of your top executives represents the degree of importance your organization places on an area of limited interest.

20. *Common Problems.* At some point during a mega-meeting virtually everyone of your top managers will be confronted with an embarrassing situation. Usually, the kind of person who makes it into the upper ranks of management can handle these moments. A little preventative maintenance, however, can result in a more hassle-free environment. Here are a few helpful insights.

  a. *Name tags.* As a rule, the longer the meeting, the fewer name tags are worn. Name tags are necessary. They help attendees talk with one another and allow your managers to recognize more participants. Use name tags as an admission badge to meeting events. Run contests to encourage name tag wear. Do what is necessary to get attendees to use them.

  b. *Alcohol.* Upper-level managers attract inebriates. That may not be a scientific rule, but you'll believe its truth after only limited experience with super-meetings. Buoyed by alcohol, some attendees cannot resist passing along their advice, condemnation, or best wishes. There is no defense against such behavior other than running interference, and keeping each incident quiet and sufficiently low-key as not to attract attention. Station one of your team next to each VIP to alert that executive. Encourage your VIPs to circulate in pairs and threesomes at events where alcohol is imbibed. And always have a security person from the hotel within calling distance of your top people.

c. *Intruders.* Large meetings seem to attract intruders. There is almost a national sport centered on crashing cocktail parties of mega-meetings to mingle, eat, and drink with the guests. Most intruders are benign freeloaders. A few are dangerous. Name tags are a defense against intrusion. Just another reason to encourage and insist on their wear.

d. *Dissidents.* Splinter groups, from within and without your organization, can create disruption and spoil the productive mood of your meeting. Dissidents come in many guises, from those concerned about an internal policy of your company to others who attack as part of an economic pressure movement on a civil government. There is a tendency for your upper management to respond freely to these individuals at the time of the disturbance. No one can talk effectively to, say, rowdy picketers in the lobby of the meeting hotel or to a group which makes a scene in the main ballroom during a social session. Keep your management away from these demonstrations. Nothing they do will help. Handle the matter through security, after making certain your top people are removed from the area.

AFTER MEETING REPORT

The party is over, the last attendee has checked out of the hotel, you and your team have enjoyed a final, relieved toast after praise from management for a job well done, and your task is complete.

Not quite. The after-meeting report is as important as any chore performed during the meeting itself. And it may be more valuable.

Ideally, the postmortem report has three parts. The first is a listing of goals established for the super-meeting and an evaluation of how well those objectives were attained. This should be a frank appraisal, and if any goals were found to be impractical, this fact should be noted to prevent the mistake from reoccurring.

The second part is composed of comments on each event which took place during the session. Comments can be yours, your staff's, and/or your management's. Both praises and curses should be included. As should suggestions dealing with how to make an event more effective. End this section with notes on the hotel or resort, covering ways to get improved service from the facilities.

The final portion of your after-meeting report is financial. Summarize costs by using ranges of prices (e.g. from $14 to $23) for rooms, meals, guests at receptions, golf costs, etc., wherever exact figures are unavailable. Show the total cost of the meeting and the original budget, with notations on items where estimates were over or under expectation. Pay special attention to expenditures for soliciting attendance, including printing and postage. End with an estimated cost per attendee.

Make the after-meeting report as short or long as you like. But make it as soon after the event as possible, while each experience, good or bad, is still recallable.

IN SUMMARY

As may be seen from this overview, planning and conducting a mega-meeting is a complex task. Yet giant meetings are held every day. And conducted, many, many times, by individuals who have no past experience. The job is more intimidating than difficult. Attention to detail is the secret. The information included here won't make you an experienced expert, but it will make the job easier. And help you avoid some common mistakes.

16 | Special Meetings

In business today, the distinction between a meeting and a presentation is blurred. Meetings used to be gatherings of individuals, empowered to debate, discuss, and/or decide on issues of mutual interest or make recommendations concerning those same issues.

That's a good working definition, but in today's working world, the word "meeting" has taken broader meaning. The purpose of this chapter is to review other types of "meetings." No manager knows when he or she might be called upon to handle or assist in one of these special- purpose activities.

AWARDS PRESENTATIONS

Properly handled, awards presentations can be a strong part of an organization's morale-development program. Are high morale and esprit de corps important? Ask any top executive. High morale is an action-productivity motivator.

However, awards presentations are not always effective. Usually, awards presentations become platforms for managers to expound on topics they feel motivate their organizations. The "awards" portion of the program is merely a device to gather people into one area, so they

can be harangued. Needless to say, this does little for building morale
or spirit. To the contrary, it destroys both.

Use the awards presentation meeting to further the behavior management desires. It's simple to do, because the way to do it is to do
little. Let the recipients of the awards speak for themselves and hold the
attention of attendees.

Follow these simple steps and you'll motivate instead of bore.

1. *Short Presentations.* Keep awards presentations short. If
there are many recipients, honor them as individuals first, members of
a group second. Even for a group award. After telling all attendees to
hold their applause until the end of the presentation, have each individual award recipient stand as names are called. Do not attempt to
hand out individual awards. Save this till later, when all others have
resumed their duties or gone home. Then give winners their certificates or other physical symbol of the award, one-on-one. It may take
more of your time, or upper management's time, but the face-to-face
personal touch is worth it. During the period of reading the award
recipient's name, display the award, in a sufficiently enlarged form, so
everyone can see it. A certificate may be turned into an overhead cell,
for example, and projected. A full-color slide may be used to show a
pin or trophy. An oversized replica may be produced. Regardless of
technique, be certain attendees see the award, the recipient, and hear
his or her name. That's the heart of the event.

Begin the meeting with a brief opening address. Do not use your
most important person. Ideally, opening remarks should be made by
a supervisor's supervisor. That is, someone one step above the level
that award winners deal with daily. This gives added prestige to the
presentation.

Opening remarks should be limited to one or two minutes. Attendees are thanked for being present. The purpose of the meeting, to
recognize outstanding achievement, is stated. The manager making
the opening comments should express his or her pride on being
present. Then the meeting should be immediately passed to the person selected to make the awards announcements. This individual may
be one of the organization's top officers, but should not be the highest
ranking officer present.

The awards presentation must also be brief. It should not be bur-
dened by a presenter's speech or preamble. The person presenting
the awards should clearly state the purpose of the award, saying what
it is for, how it is attained, and that only the best performers receive it.
The award should be on display during this statement, so attendees
associate a visual picture of the award with the honoree(s).

If the number of recipients is sufficiently small to allow for personal presentations, when these are done, the keynote speaker, who must be the highest ranking executive available to attend, should immediately take over the meeting. If the number of recipients is too great for personal presentation, all should remain standing until everyone is recognized, then after receiving applause and being asked to wait until after the program for personal presentation, the keynote speaker should take control.

The keynote talk should not exceed three minutes. Short speeches of themselves do not build morale. They may not dampen spirit as much as long talks, but it's not short duration which heightens morale. The speech should be short so that the speaker must stick to the subject, which is to congratulate award recipients. Too often there is a tendency to dangle the performance of those who have been recognized like a carrot in front of the group. The hope, apparently, is that all present will compare their actions to those of the winners. You want comparisons made, but it's the wrong way to achieve this worthy goal.

Congratulate the award recipients. Laud their performance. Thank them sincerely for their extra effort. Then adjourn the session.

That's it. Once congratulations, praise, and sincere thanks have been given, the meeting is over. Not counting the private personal presentation, which follows if there are too many recipients to be recognized individually.

What has just been outlined is a short, complete presentation with more potential for motivation than you can imagine. The trick is in the orientation of the program. It actually honors the honorees, instead of using them as an excuse to address the audience.

2. *Awards on Hand.* If the award is a certificate, have the certificates present at the meeting. If the award is a pin, have the pins there, so when the recipients leave, they are wearing them. Don't hold an award meeting without the awards. Simple, huh? Okay, but why is there an award meeting every working day in which the awards are not present? There is no rational explanation. Don't be guilty of this.

3. *Awards on Display.* Display the award. An award given then hidden away isn't nearly as valuable as an award given and displayed. That's easy to understand, too. Then why are certificates passed out like sheets of paper? A framed certificate will be displayed. A sheet of paper vanishes into an album or a drawer.

Pins are great awards. They get worn and are therefore visible. Long-term reminders of the need for excellence in a given area. Rings are effective for the same reason.

Keep the awards ceremony short, use it to honor and thank the award recipients. Let that motivate the attendees. Have the awards on hand. And give awards which can be displayed. All of that is easy to say, but apparently hard to accomplish.

ANNUAL COMPANY OR CORPORATE MEETINGS

Meetings required by law, such as the annual stockholder's meeting of a corporation, are defined by statute and practice. There isn't much deviation possible or desirable, especially from the organization's point of view. If a company slips into the habit of self-praise during these sessions, it invites outside criticism for any shortcomings or failures. The tendency is to use this type meeting as a public relations tool. Which is fine; it's just done wrong by most who try to do so.

INCREASED PUBLIC RELATIONS VALUE

Run the meeting in a businesslike manner. Follow the standard outline for these sessions, including call to order, roll call to ensure presence of a majority or quorum, reading and approval of minutes of the last meeting, consideration of the treasurer's report, review of old business, opening the floor for new business including any nominations necessary, and, if desired, having a brief president's report. Then adjourn. Take care of the business of the day with a minimum of talk or discussion.

Once the meeting is over, hold a press conference and distribute printed statements about the organization, its profit, loss, successes, and other newsworthy considerations. Even if a press conference is not held, distribute printed press releases after the session.

Keep the meeting short, to the point, and simple, which minimizes interruptions. Then, in an informal session afterwards, which has a different legal and emotional nuance, answer questions of the press as well as stockholders. Don't blend the required formal shareholders' meeting into your shareholder relations package. Take care of that afterwards. It makes life simpler.

SALES TRAINING AND NEW PRODUCT PRESENTATIONS

Sales-training sessions, including the similar new product presentation meeting, are a special class of organizational get-together which can often be used to achieve more than the stated purpose. Especially by organizations with a sales staff covering a broad geographic territory.

The common cry among branch operations, whether it is a full-fledged branch office with 50 people or a single salesperson operating from an apartment, is that the "home" office does not understand local problems. In truth, this is often the case. The difficulty, however, is usually one of communications, imagination, and scope of operations. The vice-president of sales in the home office sees travel expenses rising at an unsatisfactory rate, so issues new directives about driving versus flying. One salesperson, in the Northeast, seldom flies. The distance between calls is too short. Another sales representative in Denver always flies. Distances are too long to drive. Both receive the same directive. One ignores it as unnecessary. The other writhes under the new restriction and knows the home office is not alert to the branch situation.

Sales training and new product presentation meetings are excellent sessions for formal/informal review of policies, for managers to receive impressions from the field and gain a new perspective, and for those in the field to obtain a better grasp of management's objectives.

The original purpose of the meeting should not be shortened. It should merely be planned as part of a larger exchange of information. There are times when holding a meeting exclusively for sales training in the field can be justified, but overall, since a good deal of money has been spent to bring the sales group together, it makes economic sense to derive more from the investment.

Frequently value isn't increased, because to do more requires more of management's time. What's not fully appreciated is that the presence of upper management is a powerful stimulus to many individuals and will cause them to be more receptive to training and more effective in exchanges. Do not waste these opportunities. Long-term, if the meeting is well handled, the outlay of money and time will produce returns.

UNUSUAL MEETINGS

In some organizations, unusual meetings have become the norm. Unusual meetings are those used for some special public-relations effort, a revitalization of the sales force, corporate public relations, development of greater supplier cooperation, better insight into customer needs, improved governmental relations, increased understanding by stock analysts of the organization's position, and similar activities.

These meetings share two common denominators. First, there is a presentation. Second, the purpose of the session is to inform and/or be informed.

These sessions are not to formulate policy or make recommendations for decisions. The meeting and presentation techniques already covered will serve well in this similar but different area. And a couple of special tips will add to your overall effectiveness in these activities.

1. *Maintain Truth of Purpose.* Tell the truth about why the meeting has been called. Don't imply to a group of customers that you have come for their input on various subjects, then turn the session into a selling situation. If you've come for information, be present for information. If you've come to sell, then sell. Be truthful about why you are there.

2. *Interest Measured by Rank.* Understand that your organization's interest in a given group or subject will be judged by the rank of participants you send to the meeting.

If your organization has strong interest in a subject, send top management to the conference. Let true organizational interest in a topic be the guide for calling a meeting in the first place. Let that same guide dictate who should attend.

3. *Confront Money Matters.* If money is involved in a meeting, everyone must know this. For some reason, talk about money, in any of its forms—owed, past due, to be charged, lost, found, previously billed, paid, not paid, and all the others—tends to cause tension in a meeting. There are two ways to avoid this. Obscuring the reason for the meeting until it's well underway is not the best choice.

If a special meeting concerns money, then you must be up-to-date on the problem or opportunity. And you want those in attendance informed, too. So if money matters in a meeting, explain this matter to everyone, long in advance, to give them ample time for preparation. Be clear when calling a meeting where money will be the top topic. Take this advice to heart.

CREATING SPECIAL MEETINGS

From time to time, managers are called upon to conduct special purpose meetings and to develop concepts for those meetings. Creating a meeting theme or central idea is not an act performed in a vacuum. Input is required from upper management to determine the purpose of the meeting, to set attainable goals, and to define a budget.

Assigned such a project, you must know what management wishes to achieve and have a grasp of how much can be spent on the session. Then you are set to act. All you need is an idea.

BORROWED INTEREST

Managers charged with creating special meeting themes tend to immediately borrow interest as opposed to conceiving an effective, custom theme. If space travel is in the news, meetings with space themes abound. If a slogan from an advertising campaign has become exceptionally popular, then variations of the slogan, none nearly as clever as the original, creep into meeting themes. (If the creative writer who wrote that hot line had the challenge of finding a theme for a special meeting, you can bet he or she wouldn't copy someone else's slogan. There would be a fresh idea.)

Borrowed interest is easy and substitutes poorly for creativity. In most cases, a manager who borrows interest has provided a good guide to the overall effectiveness of the special meeting itself. It won't be great.

MEETING IDEAS

There are no set rules on the generation of meeting concepts. A good idea is a good idea, no matter from whence it comes. Remember that in creating meeting concepts, the appeal is likely not to be directed towards a mass audience. Usually, the meeting is aimed at a segment of people who share a common interest. So the meeting theme may appear rather dim to those not sharing that common interest.

Famous quotations are a good source for meeting themes. An example would be the use of Shakespeare's famous line, "Out, damned spot!" from Macbeth, to introduce a new range of cleaning equipment, a do-it-yourself rug steam-cleaner, or other items used in the spotting or cleaning trade. "Home is the sailor, home from sea, And the hunter home from the hill." Underwoods, *Requiem* might fit well with fishing and camping equipment. A good book on quotations offers an index by subject and you may discover the exact line you need to give your special meeting theme a boost.

The concept does not have to be humorous. Although humor does not hurt most concepts, occasionally it can be in bad taste. Go with light humor, eschew bad taste.

History is another source for meeting concepts. A new plastic pipe with unique characteristics might be presented in a session called simply: "The History of Pipe, from Clay to Today." A line like that wouldn't fill any stadium to the bleacher seats, but it would interest those who buy and use various kinds of pipe.

Technical journals or trade newspapers and magazines offer other sources of creative inspiration. Many articles have themes and often those themes are expressed in the article title. Don't be afraid to steal a line and adapt it to your specific uses. Plagiarism is fair in the development of a concept for a special meeting.

Once you begin seeking a theme, many ideas will come to you. Don't take the first one. Or the second. It might turn out those are the best, but even so, give yourself some choice. When you've got half a dozen, pick two. Think about them. Chances are, because you've begun the seeking process, more will follow.

Do not evaluate concepts as they occur. All you achieve is to halt the flow of thought which generates them. Get the ideas. Then evaluate. Carefully. Be especially watchful for nuances or slurs which may be derived from your concept. If you can find a hidden or double meaning in a concept, bet that someone else will, too.

UNUSUAL MEETING SETTINGS

Often, special-meeting concepts are based on unique locations. Unusual meetings can be unusually effective in unexpected locations. Many of these "unexpected" locations are willing to rent or offer space for meetings but haven't been asked. Use your imagination to associate a locale with a message which attains your meeting goals.

Kennedy Space Center in Florida might be an exciting place for a new high technology industrial product; the local fine arts museum, ideal for a cosmetic or perfume; a well-known music and dance spot for audiophile products, and so on.

Interesting locations promote attendance, lend a unique air to your meeting, and can make the meeting more productive. Use your imagination. Ideas are all around you. All you need to do is look.

17 | Test Your Meeting Skills

$\mathbf{T}$hese ten questions are designed to reveal your understanding of the techniques for improving meetings. The answers, along with a few comments, follow. There are no grades. You'll know how well you did. This is a self-test to help you determine any areas in which you need extra review. Spend a minute on each question, answer, and move on. Some may look like yes/no or true/false questions. They are not.

QUESTIONS

1. Should a meeting start on time? Even if the key players are not present?

2. Describe a good meeting room. Are participants in a meeting isolated from their everyday routines?

3. Who should attend meetings? Is attendance by invitation only?

4. When is it best to go into a meeting without a clear understanding of what you want from that meeting?

5. What is a "meeting memo?" How is it used?

6. "It's just plain foolish to have agendas, even informal ones, for most small meetings." Is that statement true, or false? Why?

7. Whoever calls the meeting is responsible for briefing those who attend. Attendees don't need advance notice about the meeting subject or do any special preparation. That's right, isn't it?

8. Minutes of a meeting, especially for small sessions of three or four, are a waste of time. Everyone who attended knows what went on. So why bother?

9. "If you're at a loss as to exactly what transpired in our last meeting, read my meeting file. It will fill you in." Is this a good idea?

10. Taking notes in a meeting is another example of wasted effort. Once a decision is made, who cares what was discussed or who said what. Do you care?

All done? Take a second to go back through your answers. Each answer is a sentence, right? No simple yes/no or true/false responses. And you answered all 10 correctly? Or maybe you didn't answer them correctly. At least you have 10 responses to the questions, don't you? Let's check the answers.

ANSWERS

1. Should a meeting start on time? Even if the key players are not present?

   Do you have to ask? Of course. Get a reputation for starting late and attendees will arrive at their leisure. Start on time, and greater effort will be made to be there on time.

   Don't want to start without your key players? Prolong the opening amenities. Take longer to check attendance, read minutes, and other tasks. Start on time. And time your start to the proper psychological moment.

2. Describe a good meeting room. Are participants in a meeting isolated from their everyday routines?

   A good meeting room is large enough to comfortably hold the number of people needed for the meeting, big enough so that projected cells or slides can be read without eyestrain or neck cramps. The room should be well ventilated, especially if smokers are present. Temperature in the space should be slightly cooler than a normal office if projection equipment is to be used.

Finally, the room should be isolated from daily operations so participants can confer without interruption. Some managers have the strange notion they can meet effectively and still handle business as usual, even to answering the telephone. Humans are capable of meeting. Humans are capable of handling routine tasks. Humans are not capable of doing the two simultaneously. Both activities suffer.

3. Who should attend meetings? Is attendance by invitation only?

Many organizations have an open-door policy. Anyone interested in a subject is welcome to attend any meeting on that subject. This approach is admirably democratic and abysmally ineffective.

The more the merrier might be a grand slogan at a dance or party, but not in a meeting. The fewer the better is a more effective homily. The only people who should attend a given meeting are those who can contribute and influence the discussion, or have an important managerial interest in its outcome.

Each attendee should be carefully selected to prevent having two or even three representatives with the exact same expertise and/or point of view on the subjects to be considered. They certainly do need to be asked or invited to attend, and should accept or reject the invitation so the group leader can seek a replacement if the response is negative.

4. When is it best to go into a meeting without a clear understanding of what you want from that meeting?

Never. If you don't know what you want going in, you are not going to get it. And if you haven't thought through what you want, you are clearly not prepared to contribute to the discussion.

Always know what you want from a session before you attend. You'll be far ahead of most of the other participants.

5. What is a "meeting memo?" How is it used?

The meeting memo is your unofficial opportunity to comment about the proceedings of a meeting to other attendees.

It's a great device for selling your position, recognizing a job well done, and bringing a group together to enhance its productivity. There are many other uses for the meeting memo. All are beneficial. It is a useful, but usually overlooked tool.

6. "It's just plain foolish to have agendas, even informal ones, for most small meetings." Is that statement true or false? Why?

An agenda requires extra effort. Someone has to decide why a meeting is necessary and what should be discussed in that meeting. Which means he or she must also have some idea that a problem exists or is impending, an opportunity is not being grasped, plans are needed, or other business situations require action.

Without a written agenda, the only person who knows the order of discussion is the person who called the meeting. Often, even that worthy doesn't know. Preparation for an agendaless meeting is ineffective, if not impossible, so overall productivity of the group is severely hampered.

You will hear managers say, "When we have a problem, we simply get together and work it out." Somehow, this informality is seen as a good management technique. It is a holdover from rugged individualism, a throwback to pioneer spirit, a wasteful practice.

Have an agenda. Even if it is scribbled on a notepad. Be certain those invited to the meeting get a copy.

Agendas are one way to get more done in less time. The few minutes it takes to write an agenda will be repaid by better participation in the meeting.

7. Whoever calls the meeting is responsible for briefing those who attend. Attendees don't need to know what the meeting will concern, nor do any special preparation. That's right, isn't it?

The person who chairs the meeting, or calls it, should have a brief opening statement which sets forth the situation to be discussed. That's a great way to get discussion started. This opening statement should be short. It is not an attempt to explain the situation in detail with all nuances. That's what the group is convened to accomplish.

If only one person in a group has an educated viewpoint of a situation, and all others in the session are not well informed on the topic, they have three choices. They can argue with insufficient knowledge to defend their positions, agree to the presented viewpoint, or leave the meeting, learn about the subject, and return, prepared for discussion.

If whoever calls the meeting is the only one prepared, knows this, and makes a strong enough opening statement to sell a point of view, that manager isn't looking for the best answer or an effective exchange. That person is using the meeting as a means of supporting his or her views. A kind of approval board. That's not the purpose of a meeting.

All invited must know why a meeting is being called, what will be discussed, and where they stand on issues. The opening statement is only a brief overview intended to begin discussion.

8. Minutes of a meeting, especially for small sessions of three or four, are a waste of time. Everyone who attended knows what went on. So why bother?

Because everyone there might not know what went on. Or might forget what went on before the same group meets again. Or might not recall an assignment and come to the next meeting unprepared. Which wastes everyone else's time.

Good Socratic teaching technique is to answer a question with a question. How many reasons are there to keep minutes? Even for small groups? This is an excellent point in time to refer back to the minutes chapter. And to encourage you to overcome the temptation not to have good minutes as a by-product of even the smallest meeting.

9. "If you're at a loss as to exactly what transpired in our last meeting, read my meeting file. It will fill you in." Is this a good idea?

Not if you keep your meeting file the way it's outlined in this manual, it isn't. It's an awful idea. Or your meeting file isn't fulfilling its function.

Your meeting file is a private document. It's your private evaluation of the meeting and individual performance. It has your comments on the leader's ability. It outlines how you feel you did in the session and how you can improve. It rates the quality of presentations made, the value of contributions, and notes the need for fence-mending. Names are used and the writing is candid. Lending your meeting file to someone should be like passing out nude photographs of yourself. Under some conditions, you might allow someone to see your meeting file, but you'd be hesitant and more than a little vulnerable. Your meeting file is a personal document. If it isn't, review its contents. Chances are, you're not being personal enough.

10. Taking notes in a meeting is another example of wasted effort. Once a decision is made, who cares what was discussed or who said what. Do you care?

You do if you're a participant and not just an attendee. Meeting notes keep track of discussions for later evaluation. They also keep track of the discussers, by showing factions, the ebb and flow of alliances, consistent positions, inconsistent positions, key managers on each side of a question, and much, much more. Meeting notes track how decisions were made or rejected, not which decisions were offered and denied. Meeting notes are a training aid in learning the art and science of productive meeting. Good meeting notes mean the note-taker is making progress.

That's the test. It wasn't hard, was it? Of course not. If you absorbed the contents of this manual, you know how to improve your performance in meetings. All you need now is practice.

18 | A Final Word

This book opens with a question. It is fitting to end with a promise.

The opening question concerns the incalculable number of hours managers devote to business meetings. Add to that the staggering total of hours spent in meetings of social, civic, and charitable groups, and the extent of meeting mania becomes apparent. Never, perhaps, have so many spent so much time so unwisely.

Yet meetings are necessary. They are part of our system of communication and are a means to focus brain power more effectively on perplexing questions.

The number of meetings is not going to diminish. In fact, with the increasing use of electronic techniques, the number of meetings will probably multiply.

It is up to you, and other managers, to see to it that even if there are more meetings, those meetings are better meetings. That's a large responsibility. Improvement will take thought and effort. Those who are able to contribute to this goal will not go unrewarded.

Individuals who can lead and direct the efforts of others towards a common goal are effective managers. One training ground and audition stage to demonstrate your abilities, is the meeting room. Improve your meeting skills and management will recognize that improvement and reward you with more responsibility. This will improve your opportunities for advancement.

Some may think or even say, "That's giving an awful lot of emphasis to meetings. They can't be all that crucial." Think about the time you spend in meetings. You cannot help but believe that improvement in your meeting skills will bring improvement to your career and to your life.

That's what this book is all about. Improving your skills so you can be a better manager and stand a better chance of moving into the top class of upper-echelon executives.

That's the closing promise. You can improve your meeting performance, which, in turn, will improve your skills as a manager.

Index